Praise for *We Deserve to Heal*

"This is the collection I have needed to read and was afraid to imagine. Astonishing in its depth and breadth of authentic feeling, thought, and intellect, this anthology is radical and restorative—like an Audre Lorde poem or an Angela Davis speech. Patrice Gopo convened a truth-telling session. There is bristling clarity, anger, compassion, and love (especially self-love) in these essays. These are the kind of writers you want as friends. They will have your back and hold your hand. Reading this anthology will change your life. Don't be surprised if, in unexpected ways, it sets you free."—Marita Golden, author of *How to Become a Black Writer: Creating and Honoring Black Stories That Matter*

"Unapologetic and frank. *We Deserve to Heal* matters because the complex, centuries-old history of relationships among Black women and white women in this country is too often reduced to platitudes and rooted in false, ahistorical notions of unity and sisterhood."—Deesha Philyaw, author of National Book Award finalist *The Secret Lives of Church Ladies*

"The *We Deserve to Heal* contributors examine race, ethnicity, gender, and misrepresentation in bold ways. The details surrounding the perils and (failed) promises explored in these stories are nuanced and interesting. With fascism and separatism threatening how we know and understand one another as human beings, this is a necessary book and conversation."—DaMaris B. Hill, author of *Breath Better Spent: Living Black Girlhood*

"Whichever side of the friendship you occupy, there is something to relate to here. *We Deserve to Heal* contains valuable advice from Black women who have taken on the roles of teacher, counselor, and savior when they just want to share honest friendships. Pay attention if moving forward to understanding is your goal."—Mary C. Curtis, *Roll Call* columnist, host of the *Equal Time* podcast, and award-winning journalist

"A powerful testimony of essays, stitched together like a quilt that offers healing for the soul and spirit. Patrice Gopo's anthology is full of authentic, honest, and vulnerable essays representing diverse perspectives and universal experiences. This book is needed to bridge the gap of sisterhood and community."—Alicia D. Williams, author of the National Book Award–longlisted *Mid-Air*

"This book aims to show us the experiences of Black women who have spent their childhoods and careers in white spaces, such as neighborhoods, friendships, and places of employment. After a lifetime of marginalization, these writers are defiantly offering us their views on systemic racism."—Monic Ductan, author of *Daughters of Muscadine: Stories*

"First, we acknowledge, then we can heal. These essays are a cry—and in some cases, a demand—for acknowledgment. In doing so, Black and white women can build relationships characterized by shared goals for gender solidarity and racial equity. These essays are so worth reading, and more importantly, discussing."—Deborah L. Plummer, author of *Some of My Friends Are . . . : The Daunting Challenges and Untapped Benefits of Cross-Racial Friendships* and founder of Getting to We, Inc.

"*We Deserve to Heal* reminds me of many conversations I've had with my sisters and sister-friends. The beauty of putting these stories down and receiving a response in black and white is giving. Gopo hints at a possible second volume. I hope to see it. This book is only the beginning."—Marcie Alvis Walker, author of *Everybody Come Alive: A Memoir in Essays*

We Deserve to Heal

WE DESERVE TO HEAL

BLACK WOMEN ON THE PERILS & PROMISES OF FRIENDSHIP WITH WHITE WOMEN

EDITED BY PATRICE GOPO

Published by The University Press of Kentucky, scholarly publisher for the Commonwealth, serving Bellarmine University, Berea College, Centre College of Kentucky, Eastern Kentucky University, The Filson Historical Society, Georgetown College, Kentucky Historical Society, Kentucky State University, Morehead State University, Murray State University, Northern Kentucky University, Simmons College, Spalding University, Transylvania University, University of Kentucky, University of Louisville, University of Pikeville, and Western Kentucky University.

Editorial and Sales Offices: The University Press of Kentucky
663 South Limestone, Lexington, Kentucky 40508-4008
www.kentuckypress.com

Cataloging-in-Publication data is available from the Library of Congress.

ISBN 978-1-9859-0349-4 (hardcover)
ISBN 978-1-9859-0350-0 (epub)
ISBN 978-1-9859-0351-7 (pdf)

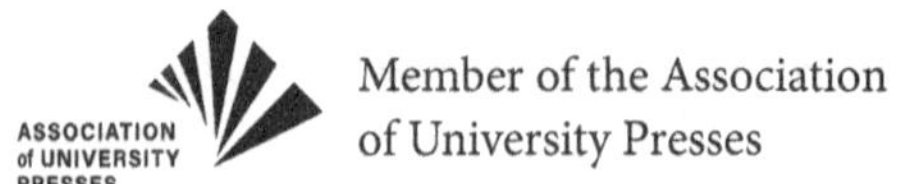

For those who have lived these words and long to heal

Contents

Introduction
Do You Want to Get Well?

Patrice Gopo

Several autumns ago, a weight began to consume me, a heaviness that left me exhaling long sighs. Until a day came in a grocery store parking lot when my body heaved with sobs. Sobs about what I couldn't even name. Around the time of my recognition of the weight, I had sat at my desk and hand-lettered words from the biblical book of John. Christ's words to the man by the pool of Bethesda: *Do you want to get well?* A question that reminded me of what I could answer each day. Below the words, I painted an image of my aloe plant, spears of green falling over the lip of a pot, stretching outward. An aloe plant. A plant that made me think of a spear split open, the fragrant juice smoothed over a burn or rash. A healing plant. *Do you want to get well?* "Yes," I said to myself as I shaded in the downstroke of each letter, creating beauty out of this singular question.

That autumn, a feeling of familiarity surged through me. *You have felt this way before. What weighs you down is not new.* Like the leaves shifting colors, my body remembered shifts in years past. With this sensation, my body asked my mind to remember as well. To sit with closed eyes, notepad nearby, a pen too. To let myself recall over a decade of autumns. To envision the moments of grief in years gone by. Each autumn for over ten years.

This anthology began with my own grief. The autumn I wept in a grocery store parking lot, I was only at the beginning of understanding the melancholy that seemed to find me midway through October each year, a melancholy that had been growing for over a decade. That October became a summons to uncover and unravel that lingering sorrow and rage. A sorrow and rage that hovered beneath the surface, somehow breaking into my everyday life each autumn as leaves changed colors and sunlight stretched into slanted gold. As I traveled back in time and relived autumns past, I ran into fractured friendships with white women. I noticed moments of goodness now gone, conflicts unresolved, points of pain, repair work that never quite remedied. These events did not color the canvas of every autumn past. However, these moments occurred more often than I had, up until that point, let myself name. To turn myself toward the past was to force myself to see both the rise of conflict and the lack of resolution. And what I saw as I looked were experiences with the power to both crush the human spirit and construct walls of bitterness.

This anthology is my response to a revelation. On an unassuming day as I followed the familiar path of my daily walk, friendship ruminations ran on an endless mental loop. My mind dwelt on situations in the past, moments of conversations gone wrong and hurts manifested; also, though, times of such joy that to remember the details became a hollow representation of all that I'd lost. At the edge of my neighborhood, as I summited the hill, a dream burst into my mind, something that I know emerged from beyond me. Rather than focusing on my own struggles in isolation, I needed to create a space for other Black women to share their stories—for them, for me, for all of us. I longed to form a community where we could see and understand what others had experienced and also be the recipients of that same grace. If it is true that one reason we tell stories is to heal, what might happen in the presence of many storytellers? This dream was a revelation. Sacred, holy, and good. *Do you want to get well?* Christ had asked the man at the pool of Bethesda—and asked me as well.

This anthology moved from abstract imagination to concrete reality because of my desire to heal. Surely, there must be a way to journey through pain but emerge with scars rather than wounds still split open. This desire led me to wonder what emotional impact Black women experience in their friendships with white women. Or if Black women can even have thriving friendships with white women despite the presence of racial brokenness. Most of all, I wanted to know if others had also experienced some aspect of what I had experienced. So, with generous support and funding from the Louisville Institute, I gathered a group of intergenerational Black women, with ages spanning five decades, with the hope of discussing and writing about our friendships with white women. I envisioned that in the act of us together sharing, we might glean new insights, find words to explain what we had been unable to explain, and affirm each other's experiences. In the act of sharing,

I hoped that we might together find pathways ushering us all toward the mending of hurting places within each of us.

This anthology is a result of that intentional gathering. At the surface, this is where Black women reflect on their friendships with white women. Even more, though, this anthology offers Black women the freedom to speak what they have lived. To speak what was beautiful alongside struggle, to pair welcome with wounds, to recognize both the perils and the promises.

What unfolds in these pages is a dialogue of sorts. Rather than everyone reflecting on their experiences in isolation, this work is a conversation as each author wrote an initial essay and also responded to another woman's essay. While the response essays take on a variety of forms and styles, at the heart of these responses is a sense of *I see you. I hear you. I see you in your story. I hear what you are saying.* In that way, for so many who have felt unseen or unheard, built into the structure of this book is truth that counters.

These conversations took on greater depth after we all gathered together in person at the Collegeville Institute in the summer of 2023. Collegeville's gracious hospitality and abundant support allowed us to commune with one another, flesh out ideas, and more fully hear and understand another person's experiences. At Collegeville, we shared conversations at dawn and at dusk. We meandered by lakes and rode to the other side of campus in an oversized van. We laughed together. We cried together. We ate together. We walked together. We danced together. We shared our individual stories and recognized the ways those individual stories were part of something greater. We formed bonds that would connect us far into the future. At Collegeville, we created a sisterhood. Some of us called that time life-changing. Others said they had never experienced such a gathering created solely for connection between Black women. I know I left Collegeville buoyed and bolstered and carrying memories that will remain with me across my life.

And later, after we had returned to our ordinary lives, I set about the work of compiling this anthology. As I read through the entirety of this completed manuscript, I noticed that we wrote in sections and parts, in metaphor and the music of language. We created forms that might contain the complexity of what we sought to communicate, and we refused to constrain ourselves to linear narratives alone. As a result of both our time together at Collegeville and this unique structure and style, what is clear is that there isn't one story for all Black women's experiences, just as there isn't one story for all of *a* Black woman's experiences. Yes, patterns emerge and connections arise, but these stories are expansive and diverse.

While this is a group comprised of many women who identify as Christians or women with adjacency to Christianity, this anthology is not inherently a faith-based book or a book explicitly for those who hold such beliefs. Instead, I mention this background because, in many instances in this book, aspects of the Christian faith shape the lens through which we view and understand our experiences. At times, this lens shapes the questions we ask, the conclusions we reach, and the laments we raise. Sometimes, we even explore the ways faith might complicate our experiences. But please know that all are welcome here. May I repeat those words: *All are welcome here.* It is my hope that these reflections capture the authenticity of who we are—inclusive of our faith—but also extend this space to anyone who wants to listen and hear.

Why the words *perils* and *promises*? What I longed for, as I stepped forth into stewarding this work, was a robust space with room for the complicated reality of friendships between Black and white women. In choosing those two words, I hoped to acknowledge that while difficulties and dangers (perils) unique to such friendships exist, beauty and goodness (promises) exist as well. I recognize that the word *promises* holds meanings that don't necessarily imply the hope for what could be. I chose the word, though, because each time I said it aloud or mulled it over, I thought of commitment and belief in possibility. So, *perils* paired with *promises* became my frame for this collection of ponderings. In the beginning, I imagined that within the essays, I might see both the perils and the promises, the struggles alongside the joy. Looking back, I know I was naïve in thinking I could flatten the nuance of such relationships to two words that I might put on opposite sides of some sort of friendship spectrum. Words are far more layered than that. People are far more layered than that, making relationships far more layered than that. Still, on the other side of compiling this shared work, I have noticed what I had deemed the perils in such relationships appeared with greater frequency than what I saw as the promises. Is this observation a reflection that, in general, perils and dangers in these relationships outweigh the promises and hope? Maybe. Maybe not. My background in public policy would suggest that I need more data to substantiate such a claim. The need to definitively answer that question, though, perhaps detracts from my speculation that the perils are what damage and harm Black women. The perils are what we often hold within and what weigh us down and enrage us. The perils are the stories we needed to tell because we longed for freedom from the impact. To contain such stories stymies liberation. So, while the joys are real and present in this collection, the struggles may feel more numerous because, as contributor Kadeisha M. Bonsu said when we gathered at Collegeville, "We deserve to heal."

In addition, working with the contributors brought me to a broader understanding of and reflection on the nature of the word *promise*. These essays challenged me to think how implicit within the formation of friendship are certain promises such as the presence of mutuality and reciprocity. Their rich ruminations encouraged me to consider what happens when such promises seem to ring false. Where I had seen *promises* as a synonym for *joy*, these essays—and my conversations with the contributors—helped me recognize how promises encompass far more meaning and uncertainty.

Given this expanding, layered, and multifaceted view of both perils and promises, it is important for me to emphasize that the essays shared here are not the only stories we could each write. But they are likely the most salient stories, the ones that carried with them the greatest urgency and need to tell. As I organized these essays, I noticed much overlap occurred between the themes in each work. Ultimately, I found all the writing together told a broader story of recognizing complicated realities, finding pathways that give life, and coming home to one's self. I hope as readers consider each of these essays, they will engage with the work of excavating both the perils and the promises present.

As a starting place for this anthology, Dorena Williamson's essay, "Turning the Tides of Friendship," considers how friendships with white women have flowed in and out of her life. She reflects that, "Just as the Ghanaian shore was an image of beauty and brokenness, so has been my journey of nearly fifty years of friendships with white women." As you read, think of the reasons friendships may have flowed in and out of your life. Then[1] Chichi Agorom explores the rage, grief, and shame that arise in her friendships with white women in her essay, "In Pursuit of a Love that Frees." She notes how the rage and grief are hers but the shame is theirs. This quote, "Sometimes, I feel like to be in relationship with white folks, I have to become a lie as well," should give us all pause as we read. What is the emotional weight of feeling like a lie in order to maintain a relationship? This question moves us into Deidra Riggs's essay, "White Women Are the Worst," where she asks readers to consider how whiteness is a mindset and dealing with white people is exhausting. Her essay's opening, "White women are the worst. How do I know? Because the next sentence I must write, should I desire to keep white people engaged, is this: Not all white women," will grip you from the very beginning.

As the anthology moves along, Kathryn V. Stanley provides needed, practical advice about ways white women can work to avoid harming Black women in her essay, "Dear White Women in Black Churches." I urge you to slow down and ponder as she asks, "Who protects us? Will our own wounds continue to remain unhealed while we tend to yours?" Next, Oluwatomisin Olayinka Oredein considers the lack of awareness white women function with in the world and how this reality harms Black women. She titles her essay, "Transparency: Observations in Tears and Terror," and gives particular, necessary attention to the nature of tears. Following these observations, Paula Owens Parker considers the gifts and limitations in her friendships with several white women in her essay, "Finding My Way." She goes on to write that these friendships "could not take me where they had never been." Then Quantrilla Ard, in her essay, "The So-Called Life of Belonging: Discovering the Concept of Friendship through a Historical Lens," draws attention to how friendships with white women and in racially homogenous spaces played a role in her journey with belonging. In time, she sees how belonging was something she brought with her and not something connected to others.

In the closing essays in the anthology, first I write about what may give rise to conflict in friendships with white women in "Seven Stones." Then, Kadeisha M. Bonsu goes on to illuminate violence at the hands of white women through microaggressions in her essay, "A Closed Forum: Q & A." She also ponders what it means to live into the tension of reconciliation over the perceived peace of reconciliation. In the essay, she asks herself—and effectively asks us as readers—the pointed question, "Why do I pursue friendship across lines of difference anyway?" And finally, the last essay of the anthology is Velynn Brown's "When You Let Go: Reflections on Misplaced Sisterhood, Double Dutch, and Other

Reasons to Drop the Rope." Here she unpacks her challenges in friendships with white women and the origins of those challenges through prose and poetry. She shares with readers the journey of becoming her own best friend and the importance of seeking out environments that embody safety, care, and joy.

As I said earlier, these essays told the stories that carried with them the greatest urgency and need to tell. There is something about the urgent stories we carry within us, a longing to let the truth of those words live beyond the informality of our thoughts and occasional conversations with others. To tell the urgent stories contained within may, in fact, be a choice to take part in what might free us from past pain and release us from bitterness that might accumulate. I sometimes wonder, though, what stories we might write now if given the opportunity to share another experience. What stories might emerge when a person has already told the story that weighs most heavily on her? The answer to this question remains, for now, unknown.[2] However, what exists in this moment are the essays here in these pages, stories that are pieces of our larger stories—far from *all* of our stories, far from our *only* stories. But here we tell these parts of our stories in order to heal from hurt *and* honor the ways we have been healing.

In this collected work of both initial essays and responses, we do not mince our words about friendships with white women. We speak boldly of loss and disappointment, pain and wounds. We explore from multiple angles topics such as mutuality, hospitality, nuanced joy, anger, shame, repair, and tears. We also ponder what it means to pursue health and wholeness, set boundaries that help us flourish, and be a friend to ourselves. Across these essays, we reside with a belief that the ability to live honestly brings authenticity and liberation and has the power to mend wounds, both named and unnamed. What began as an opportunity to share our stories became a place where the words galvanized us to release weights as we wrote our truths. And with truth comes liberation.

For months, I delayed writing this introduction as I was unsure what I wanted to say. What I now find vital to communicate is that I began this project with a hope of building a place to share parts of what I have lived while inviting others to share parts of what they have lived as well. Somewhere in my mind, I harbored a belief that freedom from patterns and behaviors and ways of being or interacting could only be found in saying the truth of an experience rather than holding it within. To share these glimpses that I and the other authors, my sister friends, have felt, known, and witnessed in their friendships would not be the end of any story—mine, theirs, or anyone picking up this collected work. Instead, I think of this book as a beginning of facing truth and carving new paths.

Did I find answers to the questions I mentioned earlier? In many ways, yes. What I realize now, though, is that somewhere along the way, the questions fell away, no longer carrying the importance they once did. Maybe I did find some answers. But what I really found was the transforming power of storytelling in community. The questions became part of what began the journey of knitting together a group of women, taking our encounters with pain and our reflections on times of goodness, and, then, turning all that into a collective something more. This process was never about uncovering answers, but instead a response to a call to convert pain into what might help us thrive.

I sit here now, and a fresh wind marks this autumn day, armfuls of leaves cloaking the cooling ground. Despite all the insights the past years have brought, I once again find those feelings of melancholy creeping into the ordinariness of my day. What has changed, however, since that day in the parking lot (and since this idea for an anthology became far more than a dream) is that I have engaged with the restorative power of storytelling in community—much like the juice of an aloe spear might soothe wounds. More than a year after I began my examination of autumns past, an unexpected moment came. As I moved through the ordinary tasks of beginning my day, familiar words from the book of John found me: *Do you want to be well?*, a version of my hand-lettered question. I discovered my answer was no longer, "Yes, yes, yes." Instead, my whispered response was, "I am healing."

Perhaps fittingly so, I write these words of introduction amid autumn, the sidewalk scattered with leaves of deepening hues, the memories of all that has transpired through this project firmly etched into my mind. The sunlight pierces pathways through tree limbs shedding stories for another year. On this autumn day that speaks of both loss and life, what was and what could be, I invite you here. Rather, *we* invite you here.

Notes

1. As mentioned earlier in this introduction, each initial essay is also paired with a response essay. While I do not mention those response essays here, please know that a response essay directly follows each initial essay.

2. Sometimes, some of the contributors and I wonder if, in the future, there might be a second volume to this work.

1

Turning the Tides of Friendship

Dorena Williamson

A Significant Shore

At first glance, it looked like any other beach around the world. Powdery sand layered beneath a backdrop of stately palm trees with their arms stretched out to the sun. I automatically took a deep breath of the sea breeze as I listened to the waves rolling in and out.

Overcome, I pressed my husband into place for an obligatory picture. I had to capture *this* moment, *this* shoreline—as if I could ever forget standing in front of Elmina Castle where enslaved Africans were dragged onto boats and forced from their homeland forever.

Those ocean waves, and many more that I've beheld, are a reflection of the duality of the sea: beautiful to gaze upon and holding perils of history; teeming with life yet depths of mystery; refreshing yet risky; a calming presence and a thunderous roar.

Just as the Ghanaian shore was an image of beauty and brokenness, so has been my journey of nearly fifty years of friendships with white women.

Navigation Lessons

The first white friendships that sailed into my world were not my own but models from my mother. In the late seventies, my parents relocated our family from Washington, D.C., to a majority-white town in Virginia. As a child, I couldn't fully know about the politics of the years following Ronald Reagan's election and the havoc it wreaked on many Black families. I just knew most of the faces at school and church were white, and they seemed to love my Black family. We shared faith; I suppose they also assumed we shared ideology since we were at "their" school and occasionally at their churches. When my baby brother was born, I remember how the white women at church constantly kissed him. Yes, he was adorable, but perhaps he was like a new pet for many white women. I mean, had they ever been up close to a Black baby before? At the majority-white church, I learned contemporary Christian songs and acclimated to a more stoic hour of church in comparison to the gospel music played in my home and the spirited longer services back home in our Black church.

My mother's friendships with white women were foundational in shaping my life and future interactions across race, and even religion and class.

A white Catholic family joined us for dinner; after my dad blessed the food, they did the sign of the cross. I had no idea what that meant but knew it was not part of my Baptist church experience. The mother of that family remained friends with my mother for decades all the way up until the daughter called with the news of her passing.

I baked chocolate chip cookies in "Aunt" Norma's kitchen, using newspapers to cool the treats. Many years later, that cross-racial baking flow would continue in my home as my daughter baked cookies with several friends, some of whom were white. Besides the sugary chocolate goodness of melt-in-your-mouth cookies, there is something very sweet about diverse children hovering over messy counters and creating memories.

I can't forget Mom's friend Mary. She belonged to a social club of Christian women who donated generous gifts of Christmas goods. To this day, when I see Orville Redenbacher popcorn in the grocery aisle, I remember the elation we felt unpacking those brown paper sacks filling our holiday table with expensive treats for our family.

Ms. Mary's daughter Wendy was a school friend and my overnight stay at their expansive home was an early indicator to my young mind that we were not from the same social class. Their home boasted white carpet that we could actually sit on as we watched television. The family had a Black maid whom Ms. Mary dropped off at home. Once, Ms. Mary could not start her station wagon, and because of her frustration, her husband went out and purchased her a new car. Our family inherited the "broken" station wagon which simply needed a minor part to repair. One family's trash became our treasure for years thereafter.

Constant As the Tide

I was active in school plays, and one time, I was asked to sing a line of the Christmas hymn "Away in a Manger" in Amharic (the language spoken in Ethiopia) for a Christmas program. I was nervous and excited to sing my line through multiple productions. I sure did bring the big "D"—DIVERSITY—bolstering the "Christmas around the world" theme. But was my Blackness valued beyond those token opportunities? At least home was filled with love, affirmation of our Black beauty, oral traditions handed down, and rich wisdom from the pages of scripture.

The difficulty of Black children occupying primarily white spaces fills me with bits of sadness like the last trickle of a wave crawling up the shore. In some of my elementary experiences, I was very aware of being one of the only Black faces. I was a jewel because I was created with infinite worth. But society has a curious way of holding us up to the light and marveling at our gifts while not fully seeing the depths of richness *because* we are Black. Having those Black spaces at home bolstered my identity against the tides of indifference and comparison. At times, my four children have also been "the only one," and I tried my best to create space for them to share their feelings and affirm their value.

Cruise Ship Relationships

Most of my friendships with white women were very much like a cruise ship vacation on the high seas: onboard for a great experience followed by goodbye and disembarkment.

Kelly and I met in elementary school and remained friends through college. We lost contact for over twenty-five years until she reached out through my website. She had come across my children's books and hoped we could connect when she and her daughter came to town for a conference. As we met for coffee, she gushed about the words and wisdom she treasured from our years of friendship. I felt a bit awkward that I did not have the same exuberance or recollection about her impact on me. As we caught up on family life and passions, it became very clear to me that we differed in our adult views on race and justice. We had shared early years of life, but our adult passions were miles apart. When Kelly glowingly mentioned her adulation of a certain "celebrity" Christian family who has caused harm to many, I felt like thick clouds of despair surrounded me. I found myself glad that our time had to end due to another appointment.

Processing this friendship takes me through file folders of possibility. Perhaps the friendship was just seasonal. Those have their place and worth. Ties that used to bind can be weakened and severed by distance and time. That is okay. But one file folder I pause in front of. (Black sisters already know where my thoughts are going.) Was I the only significant Black friend Kelly had? She was one of many white friends who spent years in my life, but I wonder if the same is true for her and Black friends. I'm at peace with the unknown.

I used to think friendships in general were all about sailing through life with laughter and time well spent. I always hoped to have lifelong friends like my mom did. As I've grown older, I believe that being together is not the sole definition of friendship. Any group of humans can co-exist in the same space and not experience friendship. How precious, though, to have your girls show up when a tsunami presents a peril in your life. The ones with whom you feel you belong, where your experience is valued; with whom differences can be respectfully and carefully held. Whatever bonds once connected me to Kelly have now evaporated into the wind, leaving bits of dusty memory. At least our last coffee reminded me that I was, and still am, wise and beneficial. My worth is not contingent on someone telling their daughter how I blessed their life. That is me being me. Giving love is its own great reward.

Treasures by the Sea

At primarily white institutions, Black students often find each other and, like magnets, stick together. But my friendship cup was also filled by white dormmates. My sister Lena's room was a haven during my freshman year of living with white roommates whose hygiene left much to be desired. Lena had one West Coast roommate who had grown up around Black folk and didn't need the typical on-ramp that new white friends needed. Our warm conversations and time together were like lovely sea shells discovered along a beach walk. I love that social media allows us to stay in touch.

I was on residence hall leadership teams with a few other endearing white friends. One was a missionary kid who grew up in Senegal, West Africa. She was the first of many white friends I've had who seemed to connect to me because their family had lived in or served on the African continent. At the time I could not comprehend, but later on, I understood that my presence in their life was an important transition point of understanding that Africans and African Americans are not the same. This learning curve would prove valuable to the multicultural work in my future. It has been quite the reckoning, realizing that white people who love African and diasporic people do not always understand or care for the reality of the African American experience.

Broken shells are still beautiful, bearing the marks of the ocean. In the same way, sharing a room with Lori was a rare and beneficial experience that shaped my collegiate years. We quickly bonded over singing, and she fell in love with Black Gospel. I can still hear her rich soprano voice doing justice to the old gospel tune "Lord, Help Me to Hold Out." I loved scooting off campus in her little sports car and learning what she loved about her family's Italian heritage. She would ask about my hairstyles and envied that I didn't have the laborious daily washing and styling work her hair required. I was ever so grateful for the ease of my hair routine: nighttime wrapping and a morning spray of oil sheen.

Lori represents the promise that non-Black girls can grow up and own the unique things about their culture while curiously and carefully learning about Black culture too.

"It's a hell of a day at sea, sir!"

My teen years included moments near the water once our family moved to Portsmouth, Virginia. When we drove the thirty minutes to Virginia Beach, I loved watching the sky change as we approached the ocean and filled our nostrils with the unmistakable smell of the sea. There were lovely oceanside prom photos, plenty of fresh seafood, and summer visits where we joined the throngs of beach tourists. I thought Virginia Beach's gray water was great until I flew to the Bahamas for a college friend's wedding. I can never forget the first sight of the blue-green swirls of the crystal Caribbean Sea. Since then, I've been blessed to see the beauty of other oceans, and inevitably I always ask myself, "Is this water as beautiful as the water in the Bahamas?"

Just like that first Caribbean Sea view became the measure of oceanic beauty, Sheila has set the standard in my life for what an affirming white friend should be. And wouldn't you know, we met at the water.

Our young kids were doing swim lessons at the local YMCA pool. Sheila recalls seeing my graphic tee and striking up a conversation. Somehow, it got around to me being the wife of a pastor, and I invited her family to visit our church. She assumed we led a Black church but still, her family showed up and remained as members for years. I got an up-close-and-personal view as Sheila unpacked her white privilege and grew a heart for justice. I walked with her white family as they adopted two Haitian daughters. To this day, I've not seen another white mom put in the same level of intense preparation as Sheila did. She inventoried what impacted her family—their bookshelves, influencers, and community—to ensure her girls would be surrounded by people of color. She gained fluency in Haitian Creole. And she diligently practiced learning to braid while waiting for the adoptions to finalize. I can admit that she does her Black girls' hair better than me! I'd like to think that I was a balm for their difficult post-adoption journey. But it was in the stormy seas of my life that Sheila proved to be so precious.

Sheila made a mean chocolate chip cookie. And she had a knack for knowing when our ministry family could use an encouraging treat. My husband and I had some squabbles counting out our cookie portions!

Beyond baking comfort, Sheila was an answer to specific prayer. When our youngest was born prematurely and needed fourteen long weeks in the NICU, I needed a village to support our family. Sheila gladly joined the circle of support by helping care for my three-year-old while I went to pump milk and bond with my fragile new baby. I cried in anguish wondering how my littlest gal was handling all the transition. Seeing the joy she had going to "Ms. Sheila's house," and how reassuring Sheila was to me week in and week out, is something I'll never forget.

Years later, my oldest son got in trouble following the wrong crowd. It was Sheila who comforted my hurting heart from the pain she endured as her own son went through a wandering season.

There will always be the hang-out friends, but the ones who show up and hold you at life's weakest points are worth more than gold.

Take Me Away

As I sift through the memories of all the friends who have sailed in and out of my life, I clearly see the white ones were, with only a few exceptions, seasonal. I was there for them; as a listener, a shoulder to cry on, and a spiritual leader. The ties that bound us were mostly faith and proximity; when distance came or when they left the church, the friendship floated away. There is a hollow place in my heart from the constant movement of people in and out of my life. My dearest friends in this life season are mostly Black and brown women with whom I share similar passions. We can talk about makeup, social justice, the pain of racism, the joys of loving good Black men, and ensuring our kids feel affirmed in who they are. This is a treasure money cannot buy.

Am I open to new friendships with white women? Despite having a handful of positive experiences, I would unapologetically be slow and careful. Hair color does not hide all the gray hair that signifies the incredible wisdom amassed in over five decades of life. I have learned to balance serving others AND loving myself—my whole, beautiful, Black self. I am entirely too old for politeness, too focused on antiracism to make time for shallow commentators or "colorblind" curious onlookers. I will not be the validation for a white friend to tack *antiracist* on. These serious times mandate that I surround myself with friends who delight in who I fully am. Who will take risks and fight for my life. And I am content that my closest inner circle is full of women of color who see my beauty like that of the ocean, who are not intimidated by my thunderous roar, and who affirm that I yet hold rich life to share.

2

Oluwatomisin's Response

Aggravations

Oluwatomisin Olayinka Oredein

water

Something about water, especially how water is experienced here, aggravates me. Its uncertainty and capacity for harm are worrying. I do not trust its capriciousness. It carries too much emotional discrepancy. It is almost like however the water feels is what the earth will know. Her waves are markers of her mercurial will, her strident temperament.

Dorena, you name the tension in a certain register for me when speaking about Elmina Castle: Water is not trustworthy, yet and still, it is an ethereal reflection of the vastness of this world and life. It is both beautiful and tragic at the same time. But, for some reason, I am fixating on its disheartening features—maybe because water feels so overwhelming. Water houses stories of curiosity and loss—curious losses, if you will. Those traversing the waters are at the mercy of its ebbs and flows. One wave can demolish a life, can change the course of someone's history. No one expects to be haunted by water, but unfortunately, many are.

By its swirling nature, water feels rageful and disconcerting. It can cause separation. For me, its volatility and wiliness are duly noted. This entity created for co-harmonious good somehow perfects self-absorption, best knows herself. She only thinks about her agenda, for her agenda is her spiraling, twisting, forcefulness.

Again, this bothers me. It feels not only rageful and chaotic, but selfish.

All that swirls around the story of Elmina severely bothers me.

The waters hold terror and tragedy within her wake. Reflecting on the movement of water, at least listening to you, Dorena, makes water an expected frivolous thing to be sure, but also the worst kind of uncertainty. Water is absolutely a source of incredible wonder, but its terror too many times outweighs that wonder. And this, to me, is quite disappointing: Water does not capitalize on how great it was created to be. It is not as kind as its surface sometimes stories itself to be.

What aggravates is that water is too concerned about water.

(water +) white women

If it is not clear at this point what the proverbial elephant in the room is here, to me, white women *feel like water*. And as the saying goes: Water will water; it will hold the potential of being more than itself but too often lurch back into the world of the beautifully tragic. It will carry but also careen. In its proposed stability, it will also be wildly unstable.

It is hard to trust this kind of precariousness. Again, the word frivolity comes to mind. Is friendship a frivolous thing, a waxing and waning venture?

Those of us skeptical of water, of white women—and especially those of us who have a shaky relationship with swimming—must flood the world with real questions:

Does the water know its potential? Does it know its damage possibility?

What and who do white women "know" besides themselves?

Does water's curving back into itself suggest a kind of malignant self-interest?

Is white women's self-saturation sufficient?

Is water even a bit curious about life beyond itself?

I am not sure that white women know to ask themselves these questions, but what I do know is that water is, in part, water because of its potential co-partners—the other elements. They all constitute the core of life's fullness.

Earth and water, wind and fire—they are most potent when together. When elements meet and make a pact, they expand beyond solo intentions. They literally change the heart of life-doing, life-creating, and life-being. But as we see in your friendships, Dorena, even if we want to be, we are not necessarily dealing with elemental alliances. We are just dealing with water.

And maybe water just wants . . . to water.

But maybe not. Maybe it wants to join-with and be-more.

The questions now turn to all of us, the other elements: What makes *us* elemental? Do *we* need water—*want* an alliance with her? Can water handle Earth's terrene, the wind's movement, fire's flare?

Does the Earth want the water in and on its flesh, fire look upon her admiringly, wind wonder what travel they can create together?

I imagine we were all created for wanting—a wanting of one another.

I imagine alliance was the Creator's expectation, but, in its painful working out, alliance has now become a distant hope.

Will water be stirred to co-exist beyond and outside of itself? At the moment, it seems like water just wants to be water. Too often, it exists ignorant that it is not that only life-changing, life-forming element of this thing called life.

It seems she does not remember she is but one part of how life abides on this plane.

(water + white women +) seasons

If water remembers, it is par for the course that water, too, can surely forget.

And I think water has forgotten—who she is and with whom she lives. Water sometimes forgets the elemental pacts required for this life-living. Everything lives with, moves with, something.

Dorena, in your moments of genial hope with these friendships with white women, with water, you see waves and seasons. Seasonal friendships. Seasons of cordiality. Seasons of hoping for something more from someones who may have no intention or capacity to give more. I, too, see seasons, but I also see something else—a spirit of reliance.

Everything is connected to something, is influenced by another. In what ways and directions this influence happens is up to each respective circumstance.

Though seemingly all-powerful and self-sufficient, water, too, can be influenced. It is the proposed balance of life's elements. Though forceful in its own right, water is not the most powerful element. It has a deference point; water genuflects.

Water will water. White women will water. And, interestingly enough, in saying such a curious thing, I see its liability.

Water must obey—*must* live in elemental harmony and cooperation, is not independent but interdependent.

Waves obey, not because they *want* to but because they have to. They are at the mercy of atmosphere. They must be in touch, in contact, in movement with the elemental forces outside of themselves. Elements can move elements.

How winds change and shift atmospheres should not be lost on us. We must not forget, water endures its own seasons, its own atmospheric encounters. Dorena, your encounters with white women illuminate how your elemental presence commanded shifts. Whether seen or unseen, your elemental essence is just as prominent as the water.

We must remember that seasons are divine crossroads where air and space and atmosphere entangle and tread, skip and eventually return to balance. Seasons are signals that the elements cohabitate the same life, that they *have to* be in conversation with one another at *some* point. Who is going to be pronounced when and to what degree is a serious question. Seasons are straightforward—a culmination of factors co-determine who shines when and whose turn it is to sit in the background.

Even water succumbs to the mercy of seasonal timing, to atmospheric graduations. In all its water-ness, it too, must reply to ambient shifts. There is another hand at play in water's story. There has always been. Water needs to remember that it exists amongst, not above.

(water + white women + seasons +) planes

Sometimes revelation comes when above.

I want to tell a story about a plane. Not a water plane, but kind of. It is about a moment of recognition in an airplane.

But first, a word on water planes. When I say *plane* I am thinking of it in two ways, first as a descriptor. When it comes to water matters, *plane* denotes the state of water. It is a surface that is even and straight.

And second, *plane* suggests a levelness. All should be even. All should be balanced. Travel along it reveals a direct line. Point A and point B live on the same trajectory. It is a straight shot; no dips and turns. For me, however, dips and turns were felt on different kind of plane.

~

Though we were going from point A to point B, the travel was not smooth.

After our time at the Collegeville Institute, one of the most rewarding experiences I've ever had with other Black women writers, Patrice and I were on the same airplane home. As you know, at Collegeville, we had all come together, were honest in ways that felt nascent and safe, and told the truth about what friendships with white women meant and did to us! Patrice had curated an experience we had never had before. Our processing was inevitable! We were on cloud nine and we showed it. Patrice and I took up air space and sonic residence processing our questions and all that just happened in excited tones and a spirit of pure curiosity. Our neighbors and others in earshot were *going to* hear about this life-changing time we had spent with one another. Our energy was inevitable.

We talked and talked, without tremble or fear. We reflected and shared and inquired, and we did so with no filter. Hushed tones were not a thought as we reflected on our nearly-a-week workshop experience with eight other fabulous Black women with whom we boldly shared stories of our friendships with white women. Though the topic was sensitive, our dialogue was pure. In that short plane ride, Patrice and I genuinely wanted to unpack what we had learned in our time together.

But the woman in front of us was water. She was getting frustrated. I could not unsee her impatience and quiet rage bubbling on the surface. There were too many elements in the room.

I saw the annoyance in how she turned her head. I saw the anger build up as she hunched her shoulders and literally covered her ears.

Our conversation was not welcome. For whatever reason, her anger stirred.

She was a dam about to burst. I foresaw the flood—the impatience, fear, defensiveness, the "just let it go, there is no problem" demeanor, the future tears. Her body spoke volumes, moved volumes.

She may not have known it, but I am fluent in water language. Many Black women are. We sense it before we even see it.

As I watched this white woman morphing, I tried to dampen the sound of my voice. I lowered my tone, hush harbored.

Patrice seemed oblivious. I am not sure if she was aware of the tension or not, but nothing changed about her. She spoke with a fullness, like she belonged on that very plane in that very seat and had the right to have this very conversation.

Seeing this, something in me woke up. I remembered what was true: Black women's words are welcome wherever we are. We can speak with our elemental force. Water will succumb, or at the very least, adjust by virtue of our boldly/bodily co-existing. Our vastness, as Black women, is just as crucial to this world as water is to the flow of life.

We Black women are privy to taking up sonic space just as much as the neighbor who wanted to idly talk about the weather or the latest news cycle. Our words are not privy to ebbs and flows, but our words shift atmospheres. Our words are part and parcel of an elemental language—they are too important to tone down.

Patrice talking at her full volume, transfixed on the intricacies of the exchange happening between us, taught me to stop being the wrong kind of translator.

Even if I heard or felt water language around me, it was not my responsibility to host it.

My only responsibility was to be in the fullness of my core self with Patrice and all her brilliance.

My only job was to be my Black-woman-self in that moment, attentive to my refusal to skim the surface of anything!

Dorena, Black women's work is not plane work. There is nothing level or easy about it. But I assure you, we will get from point A to point B.

(water + white women + seasons + planes +) wonder

We are the most important actors in the events of our lives. I think this is one lesson, Dorena.

Black women direct the winds of our own lives; our potential connections—those "friends"—do not have that power, do not possess that amount of force. What white women do or do not do may impact us, but they do not determine us. Friendships with white women are as fickle as the tide, but as consistent as the seasons. In the course of making friends, there will always be a change.

It is up to us as Black women to exist in a state of awareness of what is while allowing space to wonder what could be—especially when it comes to self-wonder. For wonder feels less binding than hope. Wonder returns us our agency—does not place into question what we did that made a dynamic change.

Wonder does not hold blame, only herself. Wonder *feels* like us—dynamic and dancing yet grounded in a sense of self; mystical and holding truth close, yet excited for possibility. It reminds us how brimming we Black women are.

And maybe this is another lesson, Dorena: What helps us *feel like us?* We need to go to whatever it is, rest in it, and speak from that space or those people. We need to live there and let friendships with white women, only the pure ones, solely be consolation prizes in this life.

We should unashamedly be our centers and, as needed, let others live by the wayside. It is OK that we are the center of our own universes. It is more than OK. It is necessary.

Once Black women focus on our loves and what we want for the heart of our lives, we exist effortlessly. We are (in) our divine element. And nothing, though it may try, can aggravate us.

3

In Pursuit of a Love That Frees

CHICHI AGOROM

Rage

I wonder what it must be like to belong to a fabricated idea and not something substantial and real. Our wise bodies always know the truth even when our heads and our hearts try to tell a different tale. Do the bodies of white people know that this identity they stake their claim on, this group they belong to, is made up, is a lie?

Sometimes, I feel that to be in relationship with white folks, I have to become a lie as well. To be clear, I do not seek out new relationships with white folks anymore. In fact, I actively avoid them when I can and have built my life over the last few years around expending my energy only in Black communities and other communities comprised of People of the Global Majority. But as a person who spent fourteen of the past seventeen years in very white-dominated spaces, I am well-acquainted with the ways in which I have had to contort myself into painful configurations just to survive whiteness. I didn't have a choice at the time. Or at least it felt to me like I had no choice since I was usually "the only" or one of a few Black folks in any space at any given time.

There is something so powerful and affirming in being able to name a shared experience, to catch someone's eye across the room who gets it, to hear someone else say, "Me too," to have someone remind you that you aren't crazy and your experiences are valid. But since I was "the only" almost everywhere I went for years at a time, I never got that experience of affirmation and understanding. Instead, I had to learn to navigate my rage and grief around Nice White Women.

One of my areas of expertise is the Enneagram. If you aren't familiar, the Enneagram is a system of nine ways of being that highlight our deepest motivations, core fears, and ways of navigating the world to ensure we have belonging, safety, and love. It reminds us that while we all have these particular habits we use as armor to protect ourselves, we are more than our survival strategies, and we can come home to the fullness of who we are.

Sometimes Enneagram teachers talk about how different cultures are characterized by a specific Enneagram type. When I think of the culture of Nice White Women, I think particularly of the Enneagram Type Two archetype. People who identify with this type believe that the world is a place in which you have to be needed or indispensable in order to be loved. The Type Two core story says, "I have to be seen as helpful and kind and generous in order to be loved." In other words, "I can't let myself be seen as selfish or needy; otherwise I will be rejected."

The thing is, Twos are naturally generous, thoughtful, kind, and helpful people. But this singular story of who they must be hardens into armor to protect themselves from rejection, disconnection, and a perceived loss of value. And while this armor serves to protect the Two, in the body of a white woman with privilege and power, that armor very easily becomes a weapon.

In my experience with white women, there is more attention and energy that goes toward maintaining a kind, selfless, "good person" image, and less attention to living in reality, especially when reality conflicts with that image. In fact, when you mention reality, no matter how gently, the Nice White Woman dissolves into perfectly cued white tears ensuring that you now have to take care of her emotions and, in doing so, enable her to remain disconnected from reality. Do you know how maddening it is to be harmed by someone's actions, and then for them to turn around and be hurt by you naming your own hurt?

I grew up in the direct and probably too-blunt culture of Lagos, Nigeria, where people told you the exact truth about yourself all the time. Sometimes the truth offered was just that individual's perception and not the actual truth, but it did give me ample practice for almost two decades in being able to hear feedback about myself, or how other people experience me, without dying. Even when that feedback stung, being raised in a culture of truth-telling meant that my first inclination was always to look for the truth in what had been shared.

This is not a muscle that white women have been required to develop. When people find out that I moved to the United States when I was seventeen, they often ask me if I experienced any culture shock. Looking back, the greatest culture shock I experienced was within my first year of college surrounded by mostly white folks. Everyone was so saccharine sweet and yet so incredibly dishonest. It felt like being forcibly spoon-fed sugar water that would inevitably make you sick later. I watched white girls smile and act like they really liked everyone in the room, and then as soon someone exited, they would talk badly about them with such comfort, as if they had been doing this their entire lives. I was in perpetual shock trying to figure out these people who used smiles and high-pitched voices to hide the truth of who they really were.

In the friend circle I left behind in Lagos, when we were mad at each other, we called a timeout and talked it out. If people within our circle had a conflict and were talking about it to others and not each other, we'd often gather everyone together and just talk it out as a group. I didn't realize it was possible for people to claim friendship without honesty until I moved to the US.

White American culture prioritizes image-management over truth-telling. American society infantilizes white women, making them the perfect little good girls that are above critique. White supremacy coddles and protects white women, giving them a terrifying amount of power that they wield with feigned innocence. And white women eat. this. up. So much so that it becomes ingrained in their own sense of self, and they genuinely believe that their motives are always good and helpful and altruistic.

In other words, our society is set up to keep white women from ever having to develop the muscle of looking at themselves critically and correctly. I do not trust people who cannot tell the truth to themselves. If you cannot be honest with yourself, you are definitely not being honest with me. So, to protect myself in relationships with white women, I swallowed the truth often. I became a lie often, saying everything was fine because I was too tired to engage this deeply ingrained belief system.

I didn't have the energy to name the harm and then be required to also console the harm-doer while they fought so hard to maintain their image of goodness. For a white woman, the world stops when she is hurt. For me, a dark-skinned Black woman, the world doesn't even acknowledge my hurt. And when I demand acknowledgment, I become the asshole. The emphasis is on how I said the thing—the delivery of it, the tone of it, how if I'd only said it differently, they'd better be able to hear it.

What I've learned now is that they don't want to hear it. It doesn't matter how gently the truth is expressed, their white feelings are immediately hurt by anything that calls into question their image of being well-intentioned and good and innocent.

I wish we could take back the phrase *intent versus impact* from white women in particular. While this is a useful life skill for all of us to hone, when it started showing up in conversations about antiracism, white women—like they often do—co-opted it as another way to protect their image of self. Something that was originally introduced into those conversations to highlight that even though white folks might not always "intend" harm, they are still responsible for the impact of their behavior, became a fun new tool for white women to say, "Even though your intention is to give me useful feedback, the impact is that you hurt my feelings, so I need everything to stop until you make me feel better."

The use of emotional fragility to get out of accountability doesn't just show up in conversations about race. It shows up everywhere because how we do one thing is how we do everything. One of my dearest friends is a white woman, one of the only ones I've remained in actual relationship with after all these years. I've watched her go through all the phases from completely unaware to developing an awareness of her own fragility and whiteness. I have had to swallow a staggering amount of truths because I didn't have the energy to manage her emotional fragility. In fact, she has told me directly that she doesn't want me to tell her the full truth. I avoided writing this essay for months because there is a part of me that wants to protect her from feeling hurt by my honesty. Not because I don't want her to be hurt, but again, because I don't have the relational energy to deal with the fallout that comes from hurting a white woman's feelings.

But where do my hurt feelings go in that kind of a relationship? Where does my anger go? Where does the truth go when there is no more space to swallow?

Interlude: Shame

What lives beneath this preoccupation with presenting and maintaining an image of niceness and helpfulness? What is the thing white women are so desperate to avoid? It's shame. The shame of being bad, of not being enough, of not doing enough. The shame of admitting that underneath the performance of altruism is the desperate need to be seen as valuable and to avoid being rejected by others. All that effort is motivated by a desire to be seen in a positive light and avoid shame and discomfort. This avoidance of shame serves to maintain the self-deception that keeps them functioning at the expense of Black folks and People of the Global Majority.

The sad reality is that the parts of ourselves we hide in order to not be rejected are the parts that we ourselves have not accepted. This is to say: White women believe shame's stories. They believe that if they are not expending all this energy and effort to be seen as good and nice and well-meaning, they are bad. Since they believe that there is a possibility that at their core they are bad, whenever I attempt to tell the truth, to offer to them a reflection of how they are actually showing up, they project their internal shame monster onto me. It's easier to make me the bad guy than to really sit with the discomfort of your own shame. I get it.

But this shame is theirs to work with, to finally stop running from, to free themselves from. Their shame is not mine to hold.

Grief

The family I grew up in could best be described as a co-working space. There was no real emotional closeness. I was the very youngest in the house, with the next person in age being either fourteen years or twenty years older than me at any given time. So, my job was to listen to what I was told and do it without complaints, to get good grades, and to stay out of the adults' way.

Friendship was the first place I felt cared for, known, and loved. It was the first place I learned that I had more to offer than just obedience. My circle of friends from middle school to high school helped me survive the emotional unavailability of my family, which is why, to this day, friendship is one of the most important things in the world to me. I mentally and emotionally commit to friends like they are my family. I'm extremely picky, and it takes a long time for anyone to make it into my most intimate circle, but once they do, it usually means I'm committed for life.

A big part of how I define *friendship* (and other loving relationships) is a willingness to risk for the other, to have skin in the game, to be committed to the other's well-being and wholeness in an active and invested way. There's a particular way in which someone choosing to inconvenience themselves to show up for me with care, presence, and support completely cracks me open. More than anything else, that feels like love to me. That is also how I try to show up in my friendships, putting effort and energy—even when inconvenient—into showing up for the other.

I've come to learn, though, that almost all of the white women I've known don't share this particular definition of friendship. They were often surprised and in awe when I showed up for them in ways that are aligned with my own understanding of friendship. They would often tell me that they have never had a friend like me, which evokes a multilayered sadness within me. It is deeply sad to know that they have only experienced themselves as deserving of care when convenient. It is also extremely sad to recognize that they will continue to show up for me based on convenience simply because it's what they are most familiar with.

It took me way too long to come to terms with the fact that the white women I knew wouldn't show up for me in the same way I showed up. They didn't have skin in the game like I did. Their version of community or friendship revolved around what was convenient for them. Even with the amount of privilege and resources available to them, the best they would offer is sympathy or a sense of shared dismay that life can be so hard.

My experience of white women has shown me that for a lot of them, care is a feeling, not an action. Support and supposed allyship are also feelings, not embodied ways of being. I think part of this is a byproduct of the culture of individualism. Within this culture of individualism, there is no understanding that our well-being is interconnected, and there is certainly no collective action taken to lessen the suffering of another. Instead, white women use their big feelings of sadness to effectively distance themselves from the situation, believing that having big feelings translates into actual care and support.

They get upset and emotional about "injustice" and "how messed up this whole system is" and how they "just can't understand why we can't all just love each other." They say these things to me with tear-filled eyes and halting breath. And that usually is the end of their care. Maybe every once in a while, they perform a gesture that helps them feel better and checks the white saviorism box. But showing up as committed, invested, with skin in the game, as an accomplice especially when there's risk involved? Well, that would be outside of the understanding of friendship for them.

For years, I thought I was asking for too much. No. For years, I was TOLD I was asking for too much from my friendships. I weighed and sifted my own beliefs about friendship, looking for where I went wrong. I tried to shrink my own desires for love and care into a smaller container that could respond with gratitude instead of discontentment when I received just a little sprinkle of care. I tried not to think about the glaring imbalance of what I brought to the table versus what I was constantly on the receiving end of.

And then, I moved away from the predominantly white geographic location I was in and created the life that I wanted in Los Angeles, with only one white friend in my sea of Black and brown friends. And that's when it hit me: I wasn't asking for too much. I was asking white women, and *they* believed I was asking for too much. White women who have been socialized from infancy to see themselves as the center of the universe do not know how to show up in a way that doesn't center themselves. Even their supposed care and "allyship" centers their fragile egos and their desire to be seen as good and altruistic by any means necessary. And when that image is threatened, they harm us in their effort to protect and maintain their Nice White Woman image.

This is where my deepest pain lies. Not in the presence of harmful rhetoric or ignorant comments about my hair or my culture, but in the absence of actual care and love. I want to be in relationship with people who are committed to me, who are willing to risk, who don't prioritize maintaining their image of being good over living and loving inside of reality with me.

When I think of the years I have spent surrounded by white women who only cared for me out of convenience, it first makes me rageful, and then the grief follows closely behind. I don't know how a white person living in the United States, enculturated into white supremacy, capitalism, and patriarchy becomes free. For so long, I thought it was my job to help them get free. Now, I prioritize freeing myself and hoping for their sakes that they, too, will one day want to be free. Freedom for me in this context looks like going where I am loved in praxis not just in theory, where people commit to me in the same way I commit to them. I hold grief for the years lost, but also deep gratitude to myself for walking away from a table where love is not being served.

4

Quantrilla's Response

The Nice White Woman

Quantrilla Ard

Hello, Nice White Woman, I see you. You've arched your eyebrows perfectly and mastered the art of the "natural" look. Your hair is parted down the middle, and your high-waisted jeans are tailored to a tee. Yet, you don't see the unraveling thread that holds your world together. I won't tug too much for fear of your undoing. That's not what I'm here for. I've come to ask questions—questions that need answers. Questions that before now I was too afraid to ask. But on behalf of all the Black women you've cast as collateral damage in your wake, I am compelled to ask. I don't require an answer really, as most of these are rhetorical in nature, and you and I both already know the answers.

As Black women, many of us can remember being taught as we grew up to adhere to a certain standard of behavior. Tell me, what is it like to not have to think about the repercussions of your behavior? To not have to immediately apologize for the words that rolled off of your tongue? We always have to carefully think about our words. Never too sharp, never too sassy, polite and kind to disarm and diffuse. We can't ever shine too brightly because, inevitably, you will attempt to douse and extinguish our flame. But not directly, because that just isn't proper. Aren't you tired, Nice White Woman?

This letter is a gentle reminder that life often isn't the way you see it—a dreamlike alternate reality in which you are the co-star. Life can be raw and gritty, a goblet of full-bodied trouble on its own without any external interference. Maybe you know this already, but I really want to call out the fact that for Black women, this often feels like one long, ongoing day, with no breaks, no time off, and no relief. With all of that, we've still managed to give grace in abundance, yet that grace doesn't seem to be reciprocated in kind. You frequently thrust upon us your mandate that we be cognizant of your time, energy, and space. We want to be free. Don't you?

When was the last time you *saw* another woman other than yourself? Not a cursory glance at her style or her hair, but a real, deep, intentional look? What about a Black woman? Did you immediately make assumptions about her hair, her style, her life? These are not trick questions, but a call to action. A renewing of your mind . . . an opportunity for self-reflection and honest truth-telling. Why do I need to qualify truth-telling with the word *honest?* Because this kind of renewal involves the real thing, not a reimagined truth of your own.

I read about your tactics, Nice White Woman. I've experienced my own interactions with your niceness when kindness would do. Do you really understand the difference? Niceness smiles when I enter the room but returns to her conversation with no further acknowledgment of my presence. Kindness, on the other hand, says hello and introduces herself. Niceness makes the teeny-tiny hairs stand up on the back of my neck. It's a visceral frustration that I can't thoroughly describe, but it is felt like the sharpest of slaps. Why niceness? Why not kindness? The shellac that Black women have had to put on to protect their emotions is exhausting. Yes, we are praised for our poise and celebrated for how well we bite our tongues, but when will it be our turn to express our angst when our spidey senses detect what my mother would call "nice-nastiness"?

Dear Nice White Woman, the attempt at befriending you has come at a high cost. A payment that some of us have chosen to default on. Some even renege on any hopes of enjoying a fruitful, mutually beneficial relationship. Still more would rather deny themselves the potential beauty of friendship with you and others like you who are allegiant to the privilege of whiteness even when it is at your own peril and to your detriment. We have played fair. We have censored ourselves. We have even put your needs above our own in a mission to make peace. But peace is not the dampening of a soul's vibrancy to elevate the other. Peace is not the sacrificing of one's sense of self in order to belong.

Don't you want to live outside the gilded cage, Nice White Woman? To be something other than a thing to be admired or coddled and handled with kid gloves? Don't you want the opportunity to live? To be your fullest and realized self? To make room for others, and in turn, make room for yourself? Aren't you tired of balancing on the pedestal? Of mindlessly being cast in the continued narrative of fragility? It is time for you to take off the rose-colored glasses that have tinted the world in the hues of your liking while you claim to be colorblind. It's past time for you to upend the preconceived notion that your value is higher than those around you. It's time for you to notice, feel, empathize, honor, hold space for, yield, affirm, confess, and own the stories in which you have been the villain and not the princess.

There are harms that cannot be undone, but there are new paths that can be carved out. The same power that was finessed for personal gain can be retooled for the benefit of all. This is a calling up rather than a calling out. It is a calling up to higher ground, emotionally and spiritually. Yet, this calling up is not to convince you to become friends with Black women (if you did, trust me you would be a changed woman), but rather a mission to reframe your position in the world. As I've heard it said, "A rising tide lifts all boats." This shift in perspective will not only realign you with how you interact with and value Black women, but women of color in general. We are not your subordinates. We are your equals in every way—made in the image of God and set aside for His purpose.

Before I go, Nice White Woman, I hope you understand that it doesn't serve either of us well to posture as enemies. It is my sincere hope that you are transformed by this and not offended. But if it offends, I understand. Sometimes truth-telling is like that. It grates on our consciousness until we are forced to change or forever remain uncomfortable. I see you, Nice White Woman, the stirring behind your eyes. You may not be ready for change, but it's here. No longer will Black women feign comfort in spaces that have not been and still are not designed for our thriving or joy. We are not pretending to "do life together" in the name of Christianity. In fact, it is in these very spaces where some of the deepest grievances and atrocities have been done in the name of the sisterhood of faith. That is not a faith that frees, loves, or justifies. That kind is a caustic and unreliable faith that ensnares and destroys the bonds of humanity.

What I do know for sure is that while you represent a large group of women who look like you, all of them do not bear this name. It is with a heart filled to the brim and overflowing with anticipatory communion and audacious longing that you, dear Nice White Woman, are able to unlock the shackles off your feet. And if you are unable to engage in the work that precedes that liberation, that is okay. Maybe one day these truths will ring in your ear from more palatable lips. Black women are tired and many are actively declining the undervalued roles of teaching/educating, shepherding, and "discipling" Nice White

Women into friendship. No more lopsided, imbalanced, painful, and misunderstood connections. The days of smiling through our tears while comforting you through yours have expired.

Humbly,
A Black Woman

~

To the Black woman who has been the "friend" to a Nice White Woman for longer than she can remember, your year of Jubilee has come. To the Black woman who has worked, lived, worshiped, and played in environments where the Nice White Woman has taken up residence, you are not in any way bound by her presence. Allow your presence to fill the rooms. Take up all the space you desire—unapologetically. You belong everywhere, Sister. The Nice White Woman sees you. She has sized you up and is threatened by the knowingness you possess. The freedom and joy that attend you, despite the challenges you face daily, make her flummoxed. She can barely believe that you are standing after all you have experienced.

Your joy is a weapon. Your brown skin is a melanated, gleaming, and constant reminder that nothing can hold you down. Your skill, your intelligence, and your fearlessness astound and amaze her. The Nice White Woman always wants to know "How?" "How did you get that job?" "How do you know that person?" "How do you live in that neighborhood?" "How did you get that invitation to *fill in the blank*?" It must be exhausting for her to bear witness to God's favor in your life despite her passive-aggressive dealings to undermine you in public or in private. To be seated at the very table where God is anointing your head with oil. It's got to be hard, Sis!

As you navigate spaces that cater to her, which can often feel like everywhere there is air, know that your presence matters and that your friendship is priceless beyond compare. The gift that you are to the world is sometimes not even visible through your own eyes. See yourself. Walk in the worthiness of love and belonging. May the pearlescence of your smile beckon the beauty that comes with relationship. May the brokenness you have felt in the past melt away like a pat of butter in a hot frying pan. May the sizzle of the pain you've experienced cool in your memory until its heat is no longer felt.

It is meat to your hungry bones to belong. And that is not something you should have to beg for, hide for, or transform for. You are uniquely you! And what you bring to the table of friendship cannot be summed up by a cursory glance at your straight, coily, kinky, or curly hair. It is the combination of your history, present, and future that makes you a gem. The Nice White Woman isn't accustomed to looking beyond the arch of her nose to find value—but that doesn't mean that she gets to assign it. Her disdain simmers under the surface of niceness but has a bite that makes you recoil every time she wields her sticky-sweet arsenic-laced words. But you, oh you, Black woman, are immune to her venom. Immunity doesn't take away the piercing of the attack. No, and many of us still bear the scars. But you, beloved daughter of God, are resistant to the potency of the very poison meant to take you out.

Let your heart remain open, despite the Nice White Woman. May each interaction be another opportunity for you to call her up to a higher level of humanity. Let your kindness be the antidote to her niceness. You get to decide how and when to enter into relationship with Nice White Women and if it is worth your time and energy. You get to relish in the care of those who value and support you. Those who hold you in high esteem regardless of your background, ethnicity, income, education, etc. Those who will not gatekeep community and friendship to check the diversity box. You deserve love, Black woman. You deserve peace and happiness and abiding connection. You deserve a soft place to land when your world is reeling. You deserve being the one who is supported as much as you support others. You deserve to be cheered for and elevated in a room of your peers. You deserve the world, Sis. You deserve it all.

Humbly,
Another Black Woman

5

White Women Are the Worst

Deidra Riggs

White women are the worst. How do I know? Because the next sentence I must write, should I desire to keep white people engaged, is this: Not all white women.

White women cannot be trusted. They don't follow through. They think only about themselves and their rights and what any and everyone owes them. They believe themselves to be weak and fragile, and badass bitches, and kind and understanding. They call themselves "*friend*" (see: blog posts, social media posts, group emails, and newsletters that begin with the words, "Hello Friend"), but their definition of friendship is way different from mine.

White women will ghost you in a heartbeat, and they will do it in the name of white Jesus. They will gaslight you and shut you down. They will steal your ideas and take the credit. They will throw you under the bus and back that bus up over you. They will not show up for you, especially when you need them the most.

They will not wield their power on your behalf. They will not follow through after posting a black square on Instagram. They are not for you for the long haul, and they definitely aren't going to show up in public for any meaningful work resulting in their own transformation or healing or accountability. They may message you privately to say they are for you, but they will not publicly use their PTO or their network or their money or their voices or their personal cache in any endeavor to elevate Black people. Not for any extended period of time. They are free to opt out, and personal freedom is a big deal to them. I have the receipts.

Is it fair to say white women are the worst? Are they? Or are they just their own special kind of evil? And . . . when I say, "evil" what am I actually referring to? Let's go with this: *Evil is anything that seeks to reverse a person's innate and divine invitation to LIVE.* White women are experts at this exact kind of evil. Policing our tone. Policing our bodies.

Policing our hair. Policing our diction. Policing our parenting. Policing our sex. Policing our fashion. Policing our lyrics. Policing our joy.

White women are disingenuous. They are backstabbers. They are self-centered, lacking self-awareness. They are fragile, abused, and delusional. They are prideful and they have impostor syndrome. They are timid, shy, fearful, insecure. They act with kindness which is not necessarily in their true character. They are hurt and broken.

> They have the power to have a young boy kidnapped,
> tortured,
> and murdered.

For whistling.

They have been taken advantage of. White women have willingly paid for and embraced a false bill of goods, which deems them fragile and needy and in need of protection, at all times and at any cost. They have a desire to know they are better than someone (anyone!), and so they convince themselves to embrace the false narrative that they are better than us.

> Boss Babes.
> Boss Ladies.
> Bossy.

Worthless Whiteness

Let me break it down a bit more for you, because there is, of course, something deeper here. The bottom line, I've come to realize, is that I expected more of white women, and they expected less of me. I believed the stories we were spoon fed about how whiteness equals superiority in all of its iterations, and I fully expected the white woman to live up to the hype.

But they don't have it in them. In truth, their whiteness is worthless.

White women have been suckling at the breast of racist tropes that cast Black women as lazy, angry, wasteful, irresponsible, money-grubbing, baby-making, incompetent, unkempt, small, distrustful, and unworthy. All that suckling has reduced them to milk-drunk, lifeless baby-women, content to be folded and propped up and decorated for adorable-to-them Instagram-worthy photo ops. *Oh, how cute are you?* they each comment to one another before scrolling on.

Despite a wish for something better, I have held out in front of me the truth of my disappointment in the white woman, my elbows locked tight to keep her at a distance. I hold this shield between me and the white woman because, as the old folks used to say, *fool me once, shame on you; fool me twice, shame on me.* I like to believe I'm no fool.

So, there's that.

Then, there is also this unvarnished truth: All people—myself included—can be, at one time or another, the absolute worst. White women, just like the rest of us, are human. And, like the rest of us, they operate in a culture where systemic racism is the air we all breathe. It just so happens that systemic racism benefits them, and therefore, there is no Great White Rush to dismantle it.

Is it reductionist to say the antagonist is always systemic racism? Do we realize how much racism is part of our existence? Do we understand just how much chattel slavery did to undo us? And not just Black us—*all* of us. Do we truly *get* the true worthlessness of whiteness?

When it comes to building friendships with white women, systemic racism has always been the antagonist. It runs so deep and has been with us for so long, that we all are so very often blissfully unaware of the degree to which systemic racism has infiltrated our cultural DNA.

When white women have disappointed me, it has always been around issues of race. Me, not feeling free or safe. Or, is it them, not feeling free or safe? Both of us, feeling blindsided by the others' response to us; to our personhood.

Without realizing it, I believed the myth I was sold via magazines and hair commercials and white Jesus. I believed whiteness was the standard to which I should aspire. It was not a thing I believed on a conscious level. It just was what it was. It was reinforced by the world around me, and I adopted this worldview before understanding completely how impotently miniscule the construct of whiteness actually is.

I do not wish to be unfair where unfairness is not warranted. It is never warranted, is it? Rather, I want to take possession of my role in a cultural juggernaut where systemic racism influences the ways in which we live and move and have our being. I advocate for myself, my ancestors, my children, and their children. I seek to be fair for us, and that fairness cannot be achieved by setting up white women as the framing support for the words on this black and white page.

My perspective is what I offer you. My experience is legit. My unapologetic existence has value.

Without Whiteness

Are you reading, believing I am referencing skin color when I write of white women? If so, might I recommend a reframing of thought, on two levels?

First, please release yourself from the constraints placed on us—you and me—as a result of racism. Remember that race is a category—a construct, if you will—created by humanity. Race was established to keep track of, to quantify, and to qualify. The construct of race exists to extol some and subjugate others. Race is like a caste system that has been birthed by rac*ism*, and whiteness sits at the top of this widely accepted yet counterfeit hierarchy. Whiteness, you see, is a (worthless) state of mind, much more than it is a physical characteristic.

Next, begin to understand *the construct of whiteness* as a central and crucial component of systemic racism. Without whiteness, the current systems of racism would fail.

You know this in your heart.

Over time and throughout history, systemic racism has had to rise up and fend off those who would seek to dethrone it as the primary operating system of cultures that confer dominance and power based on the color of a person's skin. The roots of systemic racism run deep and all facets of the system function for the purpose of protecting whiteness.

> "White America" is a syndicate arrayed to protect its exclusive power to dominate and control our bodies. Sometimes this power is direct (lynching), and sometimes it is insidious (redlining). But however it appears, the power of domination and exclusion is central to the belief in being white, and without it, "white people" would cease to exist for want of reasons.[1]

Systems Theory teaches us that when one person in the system changes, the entire system changes. Life teaches us that the only person we can change is ourselves.

Will it be strange for me to say, in a book about friendships with white women, that I don't have any white friends? Yes, I have friends with light skin, straight hair, blue eyes, European ancestry that can be traced back to the Mayflower and beyond. But they are not white.

That is not to say, "I don't see color." I do. I see it. It's the reason I put up my shield and lock out my elbows. I see color and my guard goes up because I have been burned too often, too consistently, and too deeply by white women to do anything other than protect myself and the people I love. Like I said, I am nobody's fool.

We Were Magic

My mom and dad met at Virginia State University. My mom saw my dad walking across the yard and said, "I'm going to marry him." And, a few years later, she did. I am their oldest child, born while my dad was stationed in Germany while serving in the United States Army. After my parents moved back to the States with me, my dad was discharged from the army, and my parents settled into civilian life, setting up house in an apartment in New Jersey.

It just so happened that Wayne, one of my dad's army buddies, lived on the floor above us, along with his wife and their new baby daughter. Our families were fast friends (and are still friends to this day). My dad and Wayne had met during one of their first days in Germany. In a sea of faces that didn't look like theirs, they found each other in the crowd, and that was that. In New Jersey, Wayne's wife Lois introduced our family to her friends, Jenny and Susan. Jenny and Lois had gone to school together, along with Susan's husband, Bill. Both Jenny and Susan had grown up wealthy and steeped in whiteness—Susan from New England and Jenny from one of the Carolinas. By the time our families met, Susan and Jenny had both come to terms with the privilege their lives had afforded them. I called them my parents' hippie friends.

It seemed as if our four families were together all the time. My mom, Jenny, Susan, and Lois practiced yoga together on Jenny's fancy living room rugs while all of us kids put together stage productions in the basement. I remember making up songs about whipping inflation now and passing the ERA. Jenny's son was always the leader, making sure we understood the true impact of racism and sexism and ableism and all the rest—as well as a ten-year-old Jewish boy could make anyone understand.

We were Black and European and Jewish and Christian and Catholic and not anything really. We were living out what our parents modeled for us. I was Black, and I was beautiful. I was smart and capable, and nothing about my amazingness surprised anyone. I was talented and inspiring. I was everything. We all were. On those nights we all got together and our parents tried to make us leave whatever house we were in to go home to the houses and neighborhoods we actually lived in, we'd all look at the grown-ups as if they were crazy. Then, we'd lay some blankets on those fancy rugs, grab a few pillows and eventually fall into peaceful sleep—one giant mass of childhood breathing in harmony on somebody's living room floor.

We were safe. We were loved. We were magic.

In those days, my neighborhood was a lot like that group of four families that hung out together, except we all were pretty solidly middle class. There were lots of kids in the neighborhood, and we ran the streets until the streetlights came on. I mean, we held it down. Our parents knew exactly where we were, at all times, because they could hear us through the open windows over the sinks in their linoleum-floored kitchens. We were up in the tops of the trees, playing jacks on back porches, jumping Double Dutch in the middle of the asphalt streets, making up songs while we ran through the sprinklers—topless for years, until some of us got called in by our mothers and told it was time to put a shirt on.

We had dark skin and light skin, blonde ponytails and cornrows. We liked Barbie and Legos and riding our bikes with no hands. We went to Roman Catholic Mass, Sunrise Service, Wednesday night Bible study, and no place in particular. Our dads drove into the city to work. Our moms called us in for lunch and brought out Kool-Aid for everyone. In the fall, we walked to school together, and we learned math and writing sitting side-by-side. I was Black, and I was beautiful. I was smart and capable, and nothing about my amazingness surprised anyone. I was talented and inspiring. I was everything. We all were.

When I was two years old, my family joined a church in our community. Our family was the only Black family in that church. Everyone else had lighter skin and descended from European ancestry. My parents didn't intend to end up at a white church, but back then, there was no internet to give them a heads up, so there we were one Sunday morning, expecting one thing, and receiving another. The pastor's name was Dr. Glenn Hanneman. He was a tall man with a pudgy middle. He wore his short-sleeved shirts tucked into his gray or black or tan or navy pants, he parted his hair on the side, he wore comfortable shoes and functional glasses. The day my family first visited the church where he served as senior pastor, Dr. Hanneman returned the favor with a visit to our home. He came into our house, sat on our furniture, ate our snacks, and didn't seem one bit bothered to be in the home of a Black family on a Sunday afternoon, circa 1966 in America.

My dad, who had not been impressed with the church service, was surprisingly impressed with this pastor. And so, we went back. Over time, we would learn that Dr. Hanneman had been an active participant in the civil rights movement and an advocate for equal rights for *all* people. I'm sure he got pushback. Pastors always get pushback when they speak the truth. But what I know is this: When Dr. Hanneman saw me, he *saw* me. I was Black, and I was beautiful. I was smart and capable and nothing about my amazingness surprised him. I was talented and inspiring. I was everything. And because he saw me, so did everyone else in that church filled with lighter skinned, straight-haired people. At least, that's how I experienced it.

I was safe. I was loved. I was magic.

In seventh grade, Alex Haley's *Roots* aired on television for an entire week in January, on ABC. I remember it being hyped up and hearing grown-ups talking about the show days before it was actually on the television. It was what used to be known as a Major Television Event. My mom debated whether to watch it. I wasn't really part of those conversations, but I can distinctly recall my mom saying she didn't want to watch anything that was going to make her hate. I will always remember that she said that. I didn't fully understand back then, before the first episode aired.

Ultimately, my mom decided to watch *Roots*. We watched it together, as a family. When I think back on it now, the main emotion I feel is weariness. (Back then, it was just the beginning, but who knew how many slave narratives we'd be inundated with in the ensuing years. *So many*. Yes, the story must be told, but it's not our *only* story.)

When I transport myself to that week in January 1977, I remember being happy to be doing something together, as a family. I remember feeling proud to see so many Black people on my television screen. Where had all these people *been* all my life? I remember thinking it could not possibly be true that one man would cut off another man's foot. I remember not believing anyone could actually be so mean to another human person.

Up to that point, the middle school I attended had been a reflection of the other spaces in my life. I felt safe. I felt loved. I felt magical.

My friends were brown and Black and light with European ancestry. We were Baptist and Catholic and Jewish and nothing in particular. When *Roots* was on television, we were all talking about it. Mostly, we reenacted the scenes where the babies were lifted toward the mystical night sky. Over and over, we reenacted it. But one day, one of my friends suggested we reenact a different image from the show. She suggested we tie a rope around my neck so I could be the slave and she could be the master. Back then, in seventh grade, I was still magic. And so was she. So, I said yes. Yes. Let's reenact that scene.

I don't remember anything actually being tied around my neck. Maybe we had a belt that we held between us? I cannot be sure. I try not to remember it at all. What I do know is there was a moment, when I was ahead of her and she was behind me, telling me where to go and what to do, and I looked back over my shoulder at her to see her laughing hysterically at the scene we were creating. When I remember that moment, my world splits wide open in slow motion, and the sound of the splitting is like what I hear outside my window on summer nights when a red fox is searching for a mate. It is haunting and piercing and achingly sad. I hear my mother saying, "I don't want to watch anything that will make me hate," and I hear the sound of magic losing its hold on us all, slithering away into the chasm between us—white her, and Black me.

We *Are* Magic

Whiteness is a state of mind. It's an exaggerated, hyperbolic sense of self that suffocates anyone else's attempt to take up their own God-given space and exhale . . . suffocates others' freedom to exercise their right to be still, and to know. Amanda Seales makes this distinction between people who live in white bodies but shun the white mindset (people who happen to be white), and white people who ascribe to the worthless and evil construct of whiteness: "People who happen to be white are people who do not adhere to the false notion that white is indicative of supremacy. . . . However, they understand that with whiteness comes privilege and so they use their privilege to give those who don't have access to it access . . . [while] white people are people who believe the notion that their skin color makes them better."[2]

Jesus said it's easier for a camel to go through the eye of a needle than it is for a rich person to get into heaven. I'm no Jesus, but I'm gonna follow his lead and say, it's easier for a white woman to post a black square on Instagram than it is for her to set down her whiteness and choose a different way to actually engage the world and those of us in it who are different from her.

Whiteness is the impetus for America's original sin. Those who still ascribe to it perpetuate evil on the people who simply want to breathe and thrive and sing and write and earn a fair wage and jump Double Dutch and worship Black Jesus and bake cornbread and practice yoga on a fancy rug and braid hair on the front stoop and put on plays in their basements and twerk on the dance floor and get home safely with a bag of Skittles and a can

of
Arizona
tea.

Black women are magic, and white women just don't *get* that. Not about themselves, and not about us.

So let me repeat myself: White women are the worst. And let me be clear and say it with my chest: Yes, *all* white women. All white women are the worst.

Let those who have ears, hear.

Notes

1. Ta-Nehisi Coates, *Between the World and Me* (New York: Spiegel & Grau, 2015), 42.

2. Paula Rogo, "Amanda Seales Hilariously Explains the Difference between White People and People Who Happen to Be White," *Essence,* October 23, 2020, https://www.essence.com/celebrity/amanda-seales-white-people-yes-girl-podcast-hbo-comedy-special/.

6

Paula's Response

White Girl, Please!

Paula Owens Parker

KAPOW! Did you feel the wind of the bullwhip crack as it zinged by your ear? That's what I felt when I read the title "White Women Are the Worst." I felt my body snap to attention. *This is going to be good*, I said to myself. I put the essay aside because I knew I needed to plan uninterrupted time to read it. I would curl up on the sofa with my favorite coffee in my favorite cup.

I ended up having to interrupt myself. I had to get up and walk around fanning myself, snapping my fingers, and screaming, "Yes! Yes! Yes!" Then I would sit down, read a little more, and have to get up again, pacing the floor. It took me forever to finish, and I had to reread it. Lawd, this woman nailed it! She cut to the chase! She pulled no punches. She said everything I have said and every Black woman I know has said too. Girlfriend was not playing.

When I told my Black women friends about this anthology project, the first reactions were "Oomph," "Whew," or "Wow," and then they said, "Please let me know when the book comes out." If I mentioned it to white women, the response was reserved with a tinge of fear.

Deidra wrote from her own personal experiences as a child and adult. She unpacked whiteness, evil, systemic racism, magic, and fragility in provocative ways that left me in a state of "ponderment" for days. What I mean by provocative ponderment was at the end of the third sentence, "Not all white women," I was immediately disappointed. *Oh no, is she backing off already? Where is she going with this?* I kept reading even though I didn't get that "not all white women" thing. I was amazed at how accurately she called white women out. She "read" them with a Webb telescope 'cause we must stay at a distance, right? She goes all the way in.

First reading: white women cannot be trusted. Check! Yes indeed. They will grin in your face, try to get in your business, and then use it against you. If you keep them at a distance, you are not a team player; you are stuck up and uncooperative. If they think you have an advantage, they will silently undermine you and take whatever it is away.

When the nonprofit I worked for was awarded a grant, White Girl reported disparaging information that cast doubt on our new program. Thinking her scheme would get the nonprofit she worked for the award, she was pissed when they returned the money to the grantor. It happened again with a class I was teaching. White Girl was upset because the students were signing up for my class instead of hers. She claimed I was teaching the same thing even though my syllabus and resources differed entirely. The real reason was that she was not a good teacher, and the students avoided her if they could. She had the rules changed so the class was permanently dropped from the school catalog. Never mind a White Girl had taught the course for years before I taught it.

Second reading: ghosting and throwing you under the bus. Lord, the tire tracks on my back! What can I say? Before the meeting, White Girl and you agree on who will say what, and when the time comes to speak up . . . silence. Then, they pull you aside after or text and say, *I agree with everything you said.* They don't realize their boss already knows they will never take the initiative to speak up. They watch from a distance with radar ears and either come over and interrupt the conversation or bring it up later.

Third reading: Deidra leans in hard, calling them evil, which certainly feels right! I love her definition of evil: "anything that seeks to reverse a person's innate and divine invitation to live." If they minded their own business, they would not have the time to police our lives, as Deidra described. They want to ride our coattails, hop off at the last minute, and jump in front like they have done something. It is a weird way for them to live; they are so busy watching our every move, thinking we will take something away from them when they should be busy making what they need.

White Girl not only takes what is yours but also gatekeeps what is not hers to have. White Girl wants our time, our skills, our ideas. If she sees us doing well, she will scheme and manipulate us to get what we have and most likely be incompetent in accomplishing what we do. White Girl doesn't want us to have anything, even when they are not equipped to do what we do.

White Girl, you don't realize that Black women have credentials you will never have; we have Black Girl Magic that you hunger for. If you can't have it, you want to suppress or, better yet, destroy it. But you can't because the Black Girl Magic is made from the Divine Spirit within Black Women. You will NEVER destroy it because it CANNOT be destroyed.

Deidra gets it all out in the first half of her essay. She has me jumping up and down with excitement because she is saying what I and many Black women think. They will read this essay and say, "Yaaaasssss!" "Say That!" "Word!" and be snapping their fingers and crying with relief that somebody has written it down with such power that it will punch you in the gut. She got it all out. She put it all out there.

She vented, and then . . . once the anger, hurt, and frustration subsided and the pent-up emotional tsunami had been spent, Deidra took me to a deeper level of provocative ponderment. Is this an example of what happens once the air is cleared and the elephant in the room is dissected with razor-blade precision, separating the marrow from the bone?

Yep! The author is spot-on in her discernment. White Girl is hurt and broken because she tries to live up to a lie. White supremacy's MANufactured lie was/is MANufactured to make money off Black bodies, especially Black women's bodies, from the perceived value of their "future increase" to their "ghost value" in the domestic cadaver trade.[1]

White Girl doesn't realize that white supremacy shapeshifts into laws and policies that hurt anyone and everyone who gets in the way. Compliance is necessary. To survive, White Girl sleeps with the enemy. They are in an awkward position. They get crumbs from Massa's table before they fall on the floor, and they think that makes them superior.

When I read that Deidra did not have any white friends, "I have friends with light skin, straight hair, blue eyes, European ancestry that can be traced back to the Mayflower and beyond. But they are not white," the first question that came to mind was, *Is she referring to Black folks passing?*

It took me a minute to realize she was talking about women who happened to have European physical traits. Deidra is skillful in defining White Girl and then describing White Girl as an illusion, a hologram, and not her true self. I could not get past it in my first reading, but she is not saying she did not see color; her friends are just women. How did they sidestep the whiteness dodgeball?

In the first episode of the film trilogy *The Matrix*, the lead character Neo was given the option of taking a red pill, which would enable him to understand what was actually occurring outside the illusion created by the Matrix, or a blue pill, which would allow him to return to experiencing only that illusion. The red and blue pills represent a choice between the willingness to learn a potentially unsettling or life-changing truth or remaining in the contented experience of ordinary reality with the blue pill.

If whiteness is a construct, to which I agree, and some of Deidra's friends who are women are physically white, what made them decide to take the red pill? Who influenced them to take the red pill? What happened? That is a story I want to know.

Like Deidra, I also believed the whiteness myth sold by magazines and hair commercials. Not white Jesus. Dad said, "How could Jesus hide in Egypt if he was white?" But the hair advertisements, definitely. I was six or seven, playing hopscotch on the sidewalk in front of our house. My dad was on the porch. I grew up in a household discussing family and Black history before the civil rights movement. I learned poems and read books by Black authors. All of my dolls were Black, and we never sent Christmas cards with white people on them. So, when I said I wish I was white, Dad, the activist and community organizer, got silent and asked calmly, "Why?" And I said, "Because I want long hair."

I had seen too many *Beautiful Hair Breck* ads in magazines. Pale white-skinned, rosy-cheeked models with blond or brunette hair flowing down their backs. Hair was a huge issue growing up. Long, straight hair was coveted. There were no wigs that looked like the texture and color of my hair. There were no beautiful braids down to the waist or the ankle like young Black women wear today.

I was breathless as I read about Deidra's experience with her girlfriend after watching the *Roots* TV series. Before I got to the end, I knew this would not finish well. Gasping for breath, I could see their magical existence slither into the chasm. I could feel her friend, who happened to be white, shapeshift into White Girl.

Her story reminded me of my sons' experience in elementary school. We moved to the neighborhood because of the school. The faculty, staff, and student body were about 60 percent white and 40 percent Black, just like the neighborhood. I was room mother for both of my sons, active in the PTA, and a field trip chaperone. Sleepovers, Thanksgiving plays, and birthday parties. It was a magical time until fifth grade graduation day. And there it was, the magic slithering down the chasm, the separation, white in one group and Black in the other. The protection and sheltering had run its course. It was time to move on to middle school, to enter the real world where my sons would not be safe and loved, and they knew it without saying anything. The world split for them that day, and I was sad and mad knowing my sons would now be seen as a threat, and the razor-blade tightrope walk for them had begun.

Is the existence we seek—for all of us to be beautiful, smart and capable, amazing, talented and inspiring, everything we are supposed to be—possible? Can we be the magic that creates liminal space to share the love life force in each of us? Can we bring into existence the sacred space for all of us to feel?

A glimmer is a tiny glint of light or the sliver of an idea. Either way, it's a sign of much more going on behind the scenes. A glimmer of light is just a little bit, maybe sneaking through the window blinds enough to make a flicker on the floor. A glimmer of an idea is just a tiny inkling of an idea.

Glimmers are little micro-moments that act like a gentle hug to our nervous system, helping us feel safe, present, and connected and moving us from that self-critical and/or culture-critical place to a more soothing place-affirming space.

Glimmers are the opposite of triggers.[2]

White Girl, did it ever occur to you that the anxiety, fear, shame, and guilt you feel were passed on to you by your ancestors? Did you know that your ancestors were routinely burned at the stake in England and Europe for religious heresy from the 1100s to 1612? That torture was an official instrument of the English government until 1640? That the famous Tower of London was, in part, a huge torture chamber? Did you know some of your ancestors were refugees fleeing imprisonment, torture, and mutilation; others were their children and grandchildren? White Girl, you need to understand why you act the way you act. You need to stop suppressing my history and uncover yours. You need to heal your trauma and stop passing it on to me!

Healing generational trauma is not easy. Acknowledging the pain from inherited trauma compounded by chronic trauma takes bravery from those who want to be healed and those who will stand with them. The only way out is through. That is where triggers are transmuted into glimmers, and trauma is transmuted into agency. Agency is power and the wherewithal to affect your future. It is having faith in your ability to handle your business. Agency is being grounded and flexible in the face of change and conflict.

This provocative ponderment says it all: Take the red pill, be the magic, be the glimmer, heal your trauma, and reclaim your agency because, as Deidra wrote, "Systems Theory teaches us that when one person in the system changes, the entire system changes. Life teaches us that the only person we can change is ourselves."

Addendum

As I wrote this essay, several Black women were in the news cycle: Sha'Carri Richardson, Simone Biles, EbonyJanice Moore, Blue Ivy Carter, and Coco Gauff. The headline for Coco Gauff brings me back to the beginning. It reads, "Coco Gauff advocated for herself in the workplace, so of course, a white woman cried."[3]

White Girl, please!

Notes

1. Diana Ramey Berry, *The Price for Their Pound of Flesh: The Value of the Enslaved, from the Womb to Grave, in the Building of a Nation* (Boston: Beacon Press, 2017), 7.

2. Lana Jelenjev, "Know Your Glimmers," NE Academy, March 26, 2023, https://www.neurodiversityeducationacademy.org/post/know-your-glimmers.

3. Monique Judge, "Coco Gauff Advocated for Herself in the Workplace, So of Course, a White Woman Cried," *TheGrio*, August 31, 2023, https://thegrio.com/2023/08/31/coco-gauff-advocated-for-herself-in-the-workplace-so-of-course-a-white-woman-cried/.

7

Dear White Women in Black Churches

Kathryn V. Stanley

Dear White Women in Black Churches:

For the past few years, I have observed you in Black church spaces and have become increasingly concerned. For example, there was an occasion during a virtual Bible study conversation about confession that one of you commented about feeling the need to apologize to your Black friends on a regular basis. I don't know if you expected people to stand up and applaud, but I'm sure you were surprised when I responded by saying, "Keep your apology if you're not willing to confront sorry systems and circumstances." Then you followed up by giving what you thought was a compliment to our congregation for being exceptional in leading the charge for liberation: that we are so different from others. I didn't see this as a compliment. What I heard instead was a deep misunderstanding of the complexity of Black church life and the age-old characterization by white folks about Black excellence as, "You're one of the good ones."

Another time, during a virtual interracial study of the book *The End of White Christian America*,[1] one of your sisters talked about how Black women need to lead the charge to "save the world." As one of the few Black faces on the screen, I didn't respond aloud though I'm sure my face said it all. Then later, she repeated herself thinking herself to be complimentary. I unmuted myself, interrupted her, and said, "Black women already carry too much of the weight of the world, and it's killing us." These experiences led me to write this open letter to you.

For Black women, the Black church has historically presented a paradox. On one hand, it has been a "soft place to land"—a place where, when the outside world didn't know our names or called us out of it, when our work clothes were designed to scrub your floors and raise your babies, we had one day of the week (perhaps two if you count

Wednesday night Bible study, choir rehearsal, or midweek service) where we could walk in wearing our finest attire, hats to boot, and be referred to with titles of respect, such as "Sister" or "Mother." You may remember the scene from *To Kill a Mockingbird* in which Scout, the young main character, visits her housekeeper Calpurnia's church.[2] Scout is amazed to see that Calpurnia and Zeebo, the town's garbage collector, have the important responsibility of lining the hymns for the congregation—that is, they call out each lyric in turn for the benefit of members who are unable to read. Art imitating life, for sure. The Black church has been a place where Black women could display a somebodiness they were denied in everyday life. The church is a place where Black women share stories, recipes, and can be our whole selves outside the gaze of white folk. Even as corporate and other doors have swung open for Black women, we still need the hush harbor of the Black church.

On the other hand, white supremacist patriarchal underpinnings have permeated the Black church—yes, even those of the prophetic tradition. This too has impacted Black women's church experience and continues to do so. It has meant that the church has also been a place where our intersectionality,[3] a place where the "double yoke" of race and gender, has been deeply felt.

Black women have experienced and continue to experience discrimination in terms of leadership positions in churches. My own grandmother is exemplary. Though the first woman licensed in the Congregational Church in the 1920s (now the United Church of Christ, known for its progressive theology), she was never ordained by the denomination despite her having planted Sunday schools which became churches throughout the Deep South.

Moreover, the Black church, not unlike predominately white ones, has been a place where sexual exploitation of girls and women has abounded and gone largely unchecked. Suffice it to say, the resulting wounds and continued wounds caused by gender oppression in the church continue to run deep for Black women.

And while Black women are still working tirelessly to right these age-old wrongs and address new ones, white women have decided to enter the doors of Black churches even as we are still trying to claim our rightful place in the pews and the pulpits. Your pandemic epiphanies, your desire to be "woke," and your eagerness to differentiate yourselves from the "Karens" of the world have led you to embrace the Black prophetic church tradition. And now that physical proximity isn't a barrier, you can Zoom into these spaces regularly and even hold membership from distances far and wide. But this artificial proximity also means you can remain cloistered in your "lily white world" with all the privileges appertaining thereto, while becoming self-congratulatory because of your connection with us. Moreover, you get to remain distant from or can selectively engage with the messiness of Black church life, while keeping a utopian 10,000-foot view of who and what we are.

You appear to want to use our space as a confessional for your white guilt—a place to apologize on behalf of all white people for centuries of wrongdoing and even those wrongs that happened yesterday. Your apology might extend to atonement. Perhaps you endeavor to join with us to "fight the good fight" to repair some of the systemic harms which continue to plague our communities. But that remains to be seen.

Unfortunately, on some level, your presence itself causes harm especially to Black women. For with your desire to take responsibility for the individual and collective sin of white people also comes your fragility. That is, because you are generally unprepared or uncomfortable talking about race, you tend to stymie conversations by privileging your discomfort over our experiences which have resulted in generational trauma. And with your fragility comes tears, and lots of them. My concern is you will expect Black women to dry your weeping eyes. I'm a living witness that there have been occasions when sharing space with you, I have been asked to stuff my own feelings so as not to make you uncomfortable. At times, I have done so willingly so as to continue to perpetrate the mythological Black superwoman whom the world so admires.

A friend of mine from seminary recently shared an experience which underscores this point. The day after Trump's election in 2016, there were lots of tears shed among both Black and white women in a classroom. Two things stood out for my friend. First, it appeared that the white women were, by and large, crying over Hillary Clinton's loss because they said through their tears, "But she was qualified." On the other hand, the Black women cried because they feared what a Trump presidency would mean for themselves, their children, the whole world even. And, my friend noticed something else: Some of the Black women held the white women as they cried despite the fact that they themselves were crying and indeed had more to lose as a result of the Trump era.

Similarly, I fear that as you display your fragility in our church, we Black women will pull out our hankies to wipe your tears just as we did for little white children whose parents wouldn't even allow us to eat at tables we set and stocked with the finest of foods—often while our own children received leftovers or went hungry altogether. I fear that as we seek to make you feel better about yourself, as we allow you to assuage your guilt, we will neglect to address our own experiences of systemic oppression both in and outside the church. And, as evidenced by voting patterns, many of your sisters couldn't care less about shaking up oppressive systems, since after all, they benefit from them, and so do you, like it or not. As evidence, more than half of white women voters supported "45" in his post-COVID, post-Floyd re-election campaign.[4]

The Bible says we are to "bear one another's burdens," but our backs are breaking because we bear so many of yours. The Bible also says we are to comfort as we have been comforted, but who comforts us? You have had the luxury of being protected by men, white and Black, and us too. The vote of the Tennessee legislature to expel the two Justins, Black men, while keeping the white woman who had engaged in similar conduct, is an example of white women's privilege and protection by white men.[5]

As I said to the woman in the book study, it's exhausting and it's literally killing us. Black maternal mortality, which is high even among college-educated Black women, for example, is linked to pregnancy-related stress which research has linked to racism both in the health-care system, and also day-to-day concerns Black women feel about the racist experiences they and their children have in the so-called "land of the free."[6]

Who protects us? Will our own wounds continue to remain unhealed while we tend to yours?

And yet, I would not be a "student" of Dr. Martin Luther King Jr. if I told you are unwelcome in this place. After all, King never lost hope that the hearts and minds of white people would change vis-a-vis Black people, especially those who profess Christ. You need only read King's "Letter from a Birmingham Jail" in which he responded to eight white clergy who told him to stop protesting segregation in Birmingham and instead to let the courts handle it.[7] While King's rebuttal spoke truth to power and chastised white moderates whom he described as being more committed to order than justice, King also maintained "infinite hope."

I wouldn't be a faithful disciple of Jesus or a "good" intergenerational preacher's daughter if I didn't extend you the hospitality which is foundational to the Judeo-Christian tradition and my own Southern-rooted home training. And, it would be faithless of me to not see any hope by your presence. So, while a part of me grieves your presence, I do so with a sense of hope. That said, I urge you to adhere to these few pieces of advice so that you step up into our space right:

1. Say less. Listen more than you speak. One of the vestiges of white supremacy is an ingrained belief that your ideas, your perspectives are God's and gods, that whiteness should be the standard by which all else is measured. To be sure, I am not a proponent of women remaining silent in the church, but I do invite you to view yourself as a participant observer. I invite you to use an aesthetic to view Black church culture in a way that does not privilege white culture. That you listen more than you speak and that you do so with curiosity, not judgment. To be sure, because white supremacy has been internalized by Black people in Black churches, you will see vestiges of white Jesus in our space; you may even see him on stained-glass windows. White Jesus has stained Black churches for sure. Watch and see.
2. Try Jesus and therapy. Please refrain from using the Black church as a therapist's couch to process your guilt about white oppression of Black folk and your role, however "innocent" or unconscious in it. Jesus said that some demonic forces can only be done away with through "prayer and fasting," and I would add therapy. Your own complicity or involvement in systems that have oppressed others is such a demonic force. While we are grateful for your "come to Jesus" revelations, the Black church is not the place to fully process the guilt and shame you may be feeling. That's what therapists are for. Besides, Black people have a hard enough time convincing ourselves that we need Jesus and therapy, that the generational trauma we've experienced since being dragged to these shores requires deep reflection and conversation with a professional trained to process our individual and collective experiences. We have our own stuff to heal. We can't afford to take on yours. Black church is not "free" therapy for you, or for us for that matter.

3. Use your access. Now that you are getting liberated from your whiteness, please use the access you have to other white folk who will never set foot in the Black church. There are those in your own family with whom you can forge tough conversations about race and racism. Talk to them about how racism, America's original sin, has had rippling effects to this very day. The conversations may get heated at Thanksgiving dinner, but put on your "big girl" panties and speak the new truths you have unearthed. Know that we are rooting for you. If a conversation seems too intimidating, start by sharing a sermon clip, book, or article. By the way, don't retraumatize us by inviting us to be part of these conversations. We need you to do your own work.
4. Give us space. You may overhear some things that make you uncomfortable. Know that we are still fighting age-old battles, still salty, enraged even about the trauma that has been perpetrated against us. And we will need space away from you to process, to yell, to cry, to cuss. Don't be offended if we may not want you around. Conversely, there are times when we don't want to be reminded of what we've been and are going through. We just want to be. We want to laugh, tell stories, and trash talk over a game of spades. We want a space where our race doesn't matter, where it is not a topic of conversation. We may not want you around then either. No offense intended. Don't worry; your invitation is never permanently reneged.

Bottomline: The space we take up is sacred. Your invitation to this sacred space is conditional. Come on in. While the table is already spread, our doors swing back on welcome hinges.

As I write to you, the world seems hell-bent on plowing down the same road. Banning books which tell the truth of our history and center those who have been othered; a world where there are enough who embrace one under whose gaze the entire country was shut down, millions of lives lost, that they are willing to give him another shot. My ability to muster any hope is surprising, causing me to wonder where my hope comes from.

In the Black church we sing a song called "This Joy I Have." One verse says, "This hope I have / the world didn't give it / the world can't take it away." My hope is sustained by these words and is also deeply rooted in the generational hope of my elders and ancestors who, as the old preachers would say, "Hoped against hope," who had the wherewithal to "keep hope alive" even in the face of death. So, while this hope I have surprises me, there is a sense in which it tracks with my historical path.

Moreover, through a few recent experiences, God has given me hope-filled glimpses. I recently attended the ministry ordination of an African American woman. After the initial "laying on of hands" ritual, a fellow Black woman minister came forward to do a special womanist anointing, inviting all of the "Sistahs" up to be a part of it. At first, only the women of color came forward. When they were in place, the minister then said, "I see some other women ministers in the congregation. Please join us." At that point, the white women clergy joined the rest of the clergy at the altar. These white women clergy had received the memo: Come when you are invited. Recognize that just like the enslaved who worshiped in hush harbors, Black women still need sacred places, tents, where we can hide even in plain sight.

The hope I experience has also been fostered by how I am choosing to show up in my most recent interactions with white women. I currently share leadership responsibilities on a staff of a school I joined recently. At my old school, two white women identified me as their Beyoncé because, in their millennial minds, she represents a strong, large-and-in-charge Black woman, one who says what needs to be said, letting the chips fall where they may. At first, I wore their characterization as a badge of honor proudly, largely because I wished I had Beyoncé's money and her legs, and because I pride myself in advocating for those who haven't found their voice. But my own legs became exhausted from that catwalk, and I realized when I needed someone to stand up for me, there wasn't any reciprocity. I stood on the stage all by myself. Conversely, the new space I entered invited me to be my authentic self. As I've walked in this new space, I have honored myself by doing just that.

On my team are two young white women who take seriously being anti-racist, especially in their work with Black children and their families. I have experienced a few personal and professional challenges over the past year. I re-grieved the loss of my dad upon the sale of his house and suffered the loss of my "fur baby" of thirteen years. I don't think any white woman in my entire life has seen more tears than these women have witnessed. They have held space for my vulnerability, remained strong during my moments of weakness, and even showed up with my favorite latte. They have held space for my insecurities in my new role without judgment. They have been my "soft place to land."

The way these women approach their work with Black families is also gratifying, refreshing even. They strive to avoid the white savior mentality that permeates so many spaces where white people work with Black children. Because they seek to understand the historic trauma of Black communities, they seek to understand my trauma. They don't assume that my age and education have exempted me from it. And while being a fifth-generation college graduate has provided a shield to some extent, my three degrees—two from PWIs—does not mean that I did not, have not, and will not experience the double yoke, that I have surmounted intersectionality.

It is my hope that they and you know that my successes come with scars. I don't wear my scars as a badge of honor. I don't buy the notion that what Black folk have experienced in America was God's providence. I believe God was and is horrified by how so-called Christians have used God's name and Word to justify centuries of wrongdoing. I believe that when I and other women succeed, we do so in spite of, not because of it all.

I wasn't sure how to close this letter, so I once again turned to Dr. King for guidance. When closing the "Letter from a Birmingham Jail," King did so apologetically, asking forgiveness from the white clergy if he in any way overstated the problem. During class discussions of this part of the letter, I would say to my middle schoolers, "Why is he apologizing? I don't think he should apologize, do you?" We'd explore various explanations for this, but never drew any conclusions. What I didn't notice was that King followed his apology to the white clergy by asking God's forgiveness if he had in any way understated the problem.

I don't feel led to seek your forgiveness, for doing so would undermine what I've said to this point. However, I do feel the need to beg God's forgiveness for times I dishonored myself, denied my own humanity to privilege yours, the times I have seen you as being made in God's likeness more than my own self, for times I kept silent when I should've spoken, for times where I chose my own comfort over my own liberation and the liberation of others, including you.

Hopefully yours,
Kathryn V. Stanley

Notes

1. Robert P. Jones, *The End of White Christian America* (Simon & Schuster, 2017).

2. For many years I taught *To Kill a Mockingbird* to my eighth graders, most of whom were African American. I exposed them to the so-called "classics" but made it a point to have my students read from their own perspective including centering the experiences of the Black characters and discussing current social justice issues such as mass incarceration.

3. *Intersectionality* is a term coined by critical race legal scholar Kimberlé Williams Crenshaw to describe discrimination based on overlapping social identities of marginalized groups.

4. According to a Pew Research survey, 53 percent of white women voted for Donald Trump in 2020, up 7 percent from 2016. This is despite the first woman of color, Vice President Kamala Harris, being on the Democratic ticket. https://www.pewresearch.org/politics/2021/06/30/behind-bidens-2020-victory/ Ruth et al. "Behind Biden's 2020 Victory," *Pew Research Center*, 30 June 2021.

5. "Tennessee lawmakers expelled by House GOP: Reps. Pearson, Jones ousted," *The Tennessean*, 6 April 2023.

6. Lottie L. Joiner, "Racism and high Black maternal mortality - Verite." *Verite News*, 10 May 2023, https://veritenews.org/2023/05/10/racism-and-high-Black-maternal-mortality/. Accessed 11 July 2023. For a fictional treatment of the topic, see B. K. Edmond, *The Quiltmaker*, 2022.

7. King's *Letter from a Birmingham Jail*, first published in 1963, is essential reading. I recently heard an author say that he believes it should replace "I Have a Dream" as the go-to King speech to be read on the King Holiday.

8

Patrice's Response

Places to Begin

PATRICE GOPO

Dear Kathryn,

A while ago, I sat in the balcony of one of Charlotte's oldest and largest Black churches. While I don't worship with this congregation, my friend's daughter's baptism brought me to those pews that day. At one point, I noticed a white man seated in the second row of the sanctuary. A few moments later, my friend nudged me and whispered, "There are a few." As the multitude of melodies and harmonies swirled through the sanctuary, I occasionally looked toward this man, saw as he swayed slightly and lifted his arms in praise. My mouth sang the verses, but my thoughts asked questions: *What brought him here today?* or maybe *What brings him here each Sunday?* And I do not have answers. I know nothing of his story or his experience in a Black congregation. The way he sat with a group, though, led me to imagine that this congregation had extended a form of welcome to him, and he felt comfortable in that pew.

And another story from a few years further in my past: When one of my daughters was young, she had a friend whose home we visited, who visited our home too. This child's mother was invested in her daughter acting as a good host. At their home, I would hear the mother tell the daughter, "Remember your guest. Why don't you ask your guest what she would like to do." The little girl would comply with her mother's words and turn toward my daughter, raising a question I couldn't hear before the two children ran off with the promise of a new game. I thought nothing of this directive until one day, when in my home, my daughter and her friend struggled to choose the next activity. My daughter's friend said, "I'm the guest. I get to choose." She stated her belief again, and I watched as her mother's lesson in hospitality twisted into the assertion of power. That day I told my daughter that she and her friend can make decisions together. She need not default to the whims of her friend.

~

Kathryn, there are sentences that stopped me in your letter and asked me to read them once and then read them again. You write, "But our backs are breaking because we bear so many of [your burdens]." You go on to say, "Who protects us? Will our own wounds continue to remain unhealed while we tend to yours?" I paused in these places, not out of confusion or an attempt to understand with greater depth. Instead because of the truth of your sentences. The image of breaking backs, the weight of carrying what was never ours to carry. And open wounds without the possibility of healing as we neglect ourselves in order to "care" for another. I see the pain, frustration, and exasperation in the words you wrote alongside boldness to delineate patterns and problems, to outline struggles and lack of support. As I'm sure many other Black women will, I also find myself feeling seen in my own moments of pain and frustration. But then, you wrote these words that stopped me once more: "I would not be a 'student' of Dr. Martin Luther King Jr. if I told you that you are unwelcome in this place" and "I wouldn't be a faithful disciple of Jesus . . . if I didn't extend you the hospitality which is foundational to the Judeo-Christian tradition." I read those sentences, I read the words you expressed later about hope, and I found myself with thoughts that mirrored yours. Despite the many sensible reasons someone could justify withholding hospitality and making someone feel unwelcome, like you, I struggle with such choices. Even as backs break and wounds fester.

Welcome and hospitality. Language that takes on gravity as I think through what I believe about those words. Immediately, I recall childhood memories of my family cleaning our home in preparation for guests. I see us vacuuming the carpet, sweeping the wooden entryway. I can feel the warm water gushing over my hands as I scrubbed the basin in the bathroom. So much of these efforts arose from my family's desire for someone entering our home to feel welcomed into our space. These actions connected with my parents' upbringing but were also bundled with their Judeo-Christian beliefs—just as you name. I think of the verse, "Do not forget to show hospitality to strangers, for by doing so some people have shown hospitality to angels without knowing it."[1] As a child, the possibility of unknown angels drew me to imagine who might be in our home without me knowing. Surely motivation for extending hospitality! But that starry-eyed imagination included a directive to show hospitality, show hospitality, show hospitality.

Your letter, though, invites me to question what happens when my extension of hospitality has the potential to expose me to harm?

Whether your intention or not, your words are a generosity given to the white women you've encountered in your church and other Black churches. Perhaps you wrote these words to be such a gift. Even more, though, I suspect you wrote these words as a form of protection for you, me, and other Black women. We know the presence of a white person in a Black space can have damaging—and potentially deadly—impact. You challenged me to consider what it means to show concern for another but to also show concern for oneself. Sometimes people can offer welcome and hospitality at the expense of care for and protection of self. They can melt healthy, needed boundaries, creating little separation between the "stranger" and "me." Imbalances of power and the reality of racial hierarchy—I know such factors create the fertile soil where these dynamics might readily take root and sprout. I can look to my own life and recognize the ways I have been prone to put the needs of white people and white women around me ahead of myself. The times I have listened to their many stories even as I was breaking inside. The moments I have overlooked hurtful statements in order to prevent their feelings of discomfort. Certainly, care for others matters, but I take inventory of my life and see these acts as perhaps rooted more in self-preservation rather than genuine care. Added to this reality, I can also look to moments with several white friends that carried with them a far different feel. I think now of the woman I have prayed with nearly every week for more than a decade, the way this pattern began first in our living rooms and migrated to a weekly phone call when she moved away. The way she has journeyed with me through living life, the hard things and the celebrations and the ordinary occurrences—and I have journeyed with her as well.

I share these experiences of absence or presence of genuine care because your advice offers boundaries. You created a suggested structure by which white women can engage with the Black church, and you've shared why these boundaries hold such importance. Yes, your words might help a white woman navigate the complexities of the Black church and their interactions with Black women in that space. But your words tell Black women that we need to create constraints for interactions such that we care for ourselves too. Such guidance might help—hopefully—prevent harm *and* promote healing. In situations where the historic and current power dynamic lacks equity, such advice is paramount to safety.

I think we both would say that in any situation, people need boundaries in interactions with others. And specifically Black woman should consider their boundaries when interacting with white woman as their lives overlap and they build friendships. Your advice suggests needed actions to motivate healthy—not harmful to self—welcome of white women in Black churches. I want to suggest that similar advice might create a healthy—not harmful to self—welcome of a white woman into a friendship with a Black woman. White women in friendships could heed your advice. *Try Jesus and Therapy* particularly stands out to me as wisdom, that a white woman should not use her Black friend to work through her growing racial awareness. I know that I value the white friends who haven't treated me like their therapist—or worse, a void to catch all their thoughts.

I look back on the friendships that have fractured, and I find myself thinking that perhaps delineating dealbreakers could have been a gift to build a stronger friendship foundation. Maybe such truth could have prevented painful disintegration. However, when I think of the strength of the friendships I have with white women that feel solid, I have never delineated dealbreakers, never indicated what might cause a friendship to fail. So, honestly, I don't know. I do know, though, that there is a white woman who has indicated that she would like to form a friendship with me. In the couple of conversations I've had with her, she states in varying ways how much we have in common, how similar we are. With each enthusiastic mention of how similar we are, how much I remind her of herself, I find myself taking a metaphorical step back from possible continued interaction. Her cries of similarity scare me and make me imagine that in the moment our paths diverge—which they already do—in that moment, she'll have built me into something I am not, a near replica of her who just happens to have a different skin color. How easily she will miss how we are not living a similar life because of her rooted belief in our sameness. She is not seeing me. Instead, she is seeing who she wants me to be for her. Could your simple piece of advice to *Say Less* help here? To listen instead to what I'm actually saying? Perhaps. This thought challenges me think of my own boundaries. Maybe it is *Say Less*, but maybe what I am understanding in this resonance is what I want is for her to recognize my own unique personhood.

Your letter celebrates the value of naming with clarity directives that might help a white woman promote healing—or at least diminish harm—as she engages with the Black church. Do I think your suggestions will address *every* challenge that might arise? Probably not. Do I think your suggestions might serve as the boundaries for *every* interaction and encounter a Black woman might have with a white woman? Again, no. Surely different situations and different people might ask for different boundaries.[2] But I do think your suggestions can become the genesis of deeper, more expansive consideration and reflection. I know I felt invited to reflect on my own boundary lines and what mattered to me in the formation of close friendships with white women, boundaries that I had perhaps not yet named. These suggestions aren't rules, but perhaps an example of the beauty of constraints. Constraints can be a gift, a way to offer a verdant, genuine welcome, not a welcome that grows frustrated and weary over time. Instead, a welcome that considers and cares for both parties because of the boundaries in place. Sometimes, I find it difficult to conceive that constraints can give way to beauty. Yet a poem or essay constrained by a particular structure or form often achieves greatness because of the boundaries in place. Maybe constraints have the capacity to move us toward a spacious place where welcome and hospitality are paired with mutuality and human flourishing.

~

As I finish these thoughts, I think of that Friday afternoon at the Collegeville Institute as you, Kadeisha, Paula, and I sat in the living room of my temporary home for those handful of days. Paula and I sat on the low couch, Kadeisha in the arm chair by one set of wall-length windows. And you in that lounge chair with the ottoman, another wall of windows giving us the brightness of afternoon. Why do I mention our placement in the room? At first, I think it matters little to note how we sat. But what I remember is that because of the way we were seated, I had to intentionally shift my body in order to see you. It was easy from my perch to see Kadeisha and Paula, but to see you seated in a chair slightly beyond my direct sight required something additional of me. So, of course, I recall that moment as Kadeisha questioned you about the words you wrote about hope, wanting to know more. I turned to look at you as you responded to her question. Now I can't remember all the words you spoke, but you referenced Dr. King's essay and said, "I don't know why I still have hope, but I do." I watched your eyes begin to water with this now spoken reality. That hope existed within you not because of some tenet of faith, some burden and requirement placed upon you. Instead, because of something you couldn't quite explain. Your eyes reddened with those tears as you voiced this puzzle. To hear you was to listen to something that perhaps exists within me too. To turn toward your voice was to turn toward the acknowledgement of what had been previously murky in my mind. That yes, I, too, still have hope, and I'm not sure why I do.

Kathryn, like you, I also need to ask God's forgiveness for the times I have denied my own humanity to privilege the humanity of a white woman. With such ease, these actions can happen and, yet, this way of being is not welcome or hospitality. Such actions go against the intended way we should be. But as you do at the end of your letter, I can also name moments where my friendships with white women displayed healthy boundaries. I close this letter with my belief that the most authentic form of welcome and hospitality—whether a Black church welcoming white women into the pews or a Black woman welcoming a white friend into friendship—is recognition that boundaries matter. Time spent identifying those boundaries can impact the trajectory of the interaction. These boundaries might serve as one avenue in which we can open ourselves to such relationships but also work to mitigate possible damage. And the presence of these boundaries might help us affirm how we all bear God's likeness in equal amounts, that our welcome need not elevate another to a position that mirrors the brokenness of hierarchy. Your advice won't solve all the issues. But it's a start. Sometimes, we just need a place to begin. And maybe places to begin present another possibility to heal broken backs and festering wounds. The healing of what is broken, this, I hope. This, I hope. This, I hope.

Thank you for your letter.

With gratitude,
Patrice

Notes

1. *Holy Bible, New International Version* (Biblica, Inc., 2011), Heb. 13:2.

2. For example, I know some of my friendships with white women thrive because of the presence of mutuality and consistency in the relationships. After experiencing fracturing due to the absence of such traits, I am aware that the presence of mutuality and consistency are particular boundaries that are important to me. I don't want to assume this is necessarily the case for everyone.

9

Transparency

Observations in Tears and Terror

Oluwatomisin Olayinka Oredein

one

I always enter into these types of relationships with caution and suspicion. In my experience, whether intentional or not, white women tend to navigate and manipulate relationships with a brutish je ne sais quoi—unchecked sensitivity, an overwhelming sense of overwhelm, a reactionism that unfortunately has consequences for Black people.

I watch them a lot as I'm interested in all that is happening within them.

They wear in their skin a melancholic, assumed powerlessness, a powerlessness constantly crashing into reservoirs of power onto which they unknowingly yet constantly cling—until their hands bleed.

I see them.

They resentfully host an internal fear, a sense of helplessness that is constantly at war with the potential of who they can be. It is like they want to forge ahead and break glass ceilings but are constantly surprised by the cuts they receive. Assumed powerlessness is confusing. It is difficult to realize that breaking through (anything) will hurt.

Their hands keep bleeding. They keep bleeding everywhere.

On everyone.

They bleed everyone.

The good ones do not mean to, but they bleed everyone.

Bloodletting still stains.

Tears stain just as bad as blood.

two

It is terrifying being in public with a white woman friend who begins to cry.

I worry about my safety.

Of course, I care about what is making her upset, but I care most about my safety.

They all do it. Cry.

But here's the thing: I pride myself on being highly selective, with befriending white women who are actually about something instead of just talking about it. But the tears always come. It is a language for them. It is a speaking from the body, which might be admirable if it did not bleed all over everyone.

Tears are bait—blood in the water—attracting the most toxic of protectors, self-appointed guardians of the defenseless. The sharks of salvation complexes.

They are meant to be therapeutic, but given tears' power, perhaps the medicinal can only be so in private (professional therapeutic settings). In public spaces, imaginary protectors lurk and presumed perpetrators are subject to toxic protection syndrome.

As always, Black people are bled (on).

Crying is how white women know how to push out their emotions, how to make their internal world matter in the world. And that is OK . . . until it isn't.

The good ones mean their tears as release, not as weapons, but toxic protectors lack basic interpretation skills. Their language is tangled in false myths of bravery and projected fears.

They have their own therapy they need to do.

Toxic protectors are sharks in the water. They smell blood. They seek those bled upon.

Even the good white women cry. They process their pain and frustration and anger in streams they don't realize are splashing onto the clothes, skin, and histories of everyone—those sitting with them, those outside the room, those who "fit the description": aggressive, firm, threatening, suspicious, tall and too sure of herself, sassy, attitudinal, eerily confident, a bit too secure—so the protectors come in haste. They, too, must secure the perimeter. They see blood . . . blood in the water.

I told you: tears stain.

three

Friend is a strong word in my lexicon. It means more than a social peer; it means someone I can trust to protect me, to speak honestly with me, who understands how to read a situation and an attitude—especially their own.

Friend includes a strong sense of self-awareness as well as awareness of another. To be my friend, one must courageously say and do something about their awareness. Awareness must transform into evolution. White women must transform away from themselves.

Many white women think the work of being attuned to something is the same as doing something about it. It is the requirement of change and growth that stunts many an interracial friendship.

All it takes is one. One mistake can throw a friendship right back into a suspicion-ship.

I know this all too well.

Moments where the multiplicity of my identity meets the simplicity of their own, things go awry. Elevating my Blackness, my Nigerian-Americanness, my liminality (this living in-between worlds), my immigrant identity reads as a betrayal to our "sisterhood."

They forget that my self-savviness, my political constitution, are requirements for living. I am well aware of the nuances of living in this body. Most of them are not. I am constantly negotiating my posture and presence so that I might stand upright at precise moments. They, oddly, see commitment contortion; they see me betraying their definition of sisterhood. To them, it's black and white: Am I with them or not?

If I am not woman just like them, they have no idea where to place me or what to make of me.

But I adjust and transform in order to have space and stature; I speak many languages. I have to.

For those whose language is tears, I am perceived as blurry.

White women have not had to be many things. They have not had to dance between cultures of oppression. They *think* they have because being non–white man requires an extra step. But extra steps do not necessarily imply knowing how the beat is working, knowing the rhythms of navigating multiple existences.

Our tongues and toes dance differently. To be *my* kind of Black woman requires I tread various waters, including seas of whiteness.

Their tears always betray the internal confusion . . . sometimes it is hard to understand what one is not.

They do not know what to make of me, oblivious to the absurdity that *they even think they can make me anything*.

White women, we are not sisters. We are same-somethings, just not sisters.

This is nothing to cry about; it is something to wo/ander into.

four

The moment where a white woman stands at the crossroads of her white womanhood and my Black womanhood, a choice is always made—and my Black womanhood, the thing that is praised and uplifted (in public) for being a space of such strength and poise, is shelved.

The white womanhood bond is too strong to resist. And to be fair, if one is white, ten times out of ten they will choose themselves, their daughters, their sisters, their grandmothers and mothers, their cousins, hell, even their neighbors. For white women, their sisterhood is a blood bond; it trumps everything and everyone else (those white women who are directly and intentionally invested in enabling toxic protectors are a slightly different story).

Even in this progressive age, the blood bond does strange magic. It undoes the undoing. It reconstructs the deconstructed. Even out of progressive (white women's) mouths, the blood bond anachronizes the world—throws everyone back into a wretched past that, ironically, progressive white women, too, have worked tirelessly to escape . . . unless their work was not in earnest, for there must be something there from which they feed, gain, and benefit.

This must be why they tap into the inherent magic of their tears—they must know there is something ancient about it that catalyzes the past.

Their tears mean something, conjure and rattle awake the insecurities and shortsightedness of toxic protectors. These tears keep structures in place we Black women thought these "friends" vowed to tear down.

Once a white woman cries, the whole world is under a spell. Once her voice shakes and wavers, the lines and boundaries of human being falter. Who is human again comes into question. Saltwater forces erase memories and reconstruct them in whiteness's own image, a snaring image many (forward-thinking) white women think they want to expand beyond, yet exist within so effortlessly.

Gender conversations be damned. We already know that toxic protectors and their minions have limited sight; they only see what they want, hear what they want. They cast damsels so they can deliver them from distress; they will always see a white woman even where white women no longer claim to exist.

Those born into the sisterhood know this.

Magic can do strange things, strong things. It can introduce the perception that something has changed before our very eyes. But if we pay close attention, the core of it is still there, can be returned (to). Natural forces are subdued by spiritual forces.

It is when we are unsure of what is natural and what is spiritual that the overall experience gets interesting, and frankly, for Black people, terrifying.

Blood bonds have ethereal implications.

five

I wonder if white women know that they are ghosts. How else do we talk about the terror of tears, the haunting howls of misery and menace?

When their faces flush, the pinkness of their countenance signals a shift in the atmosphere—it is like seeing a ghost. Their breathing changes, shortening and quickening—almost as if a spirit is trying to shout out something. Saltwater crowds the surface drowning out any possibility of mutuality; the listening is over. White women's upset is a paranormal event.

I wonder if white women know that the routes and avenues of their feelings carry spiritual entities—that saltwater inbreaking releases forces of repression and oppression that attach themselves to Black chests and psyches. Tears are not only floodgates or bloodgates; they also let something else in. Or, perhaps out.

Do they know?

Are they aware they are hurting those of us who do not share their sisterhood in their raw moment of expressing hurt?

Tears hurt. Tears are hurting.

Shrills that stain, bloodcurdling screams—their ghost song unrecognizable to those who are just trying to live. All we know is the terror.

I wonder if they know how the terror feels. Does this terror mimic the angry outbursts of toxic protectors for them? Honestly, I don't know, for even *that* feels different for both of us. Toxic outbursts haunt and castigate.

Are ghosts aware that they are ghosts? That they have unfinished business that haunts others until there is resolution? But what is resolution to the self-concerned? Privileged oppression is hardly talked about, certainly not haunted about.

Do specters know that when they speak their language, they create spectators and seekers—people overwhelmed by dread, searching in desperation to make the cacophony stop, so that they won't get lost in translation?

Are ghosts aware of how they make others feel? Or are their feelings too mighty a foe to fall?

What exactly is ghost-feeling but elusive regret (remorse that they just cannot quite put their finger on)?

Do ghosts know what they are made of and what they are making? Do they know the substance of themselves?

six

I imagine that being a white woman with some semblance of awareness must create an eternal existential crisis. It seems that white women are still learning themselves, thus it may be ambitious of me to expect them to be what I consider a good friend.

If I am completely honest, I don't think many white women have figured out what their aliveness should feel like. Maybe some aliveness can be found in the tears, but such a release has so much haunt to it and hate in it that I doubt tears invite life.

The elusiveness must be maddening: What gives white women life or joy if they are *even slightly* aware of the apocalypse their stains can cause?

If their life is a constant learning, or a painful enlightenment, or a consistent mourning, when is there space for simply being?

What does it mean to *be* a white woman, one of the good ones?

To know the extent of harm the imaging of your life has caused must weigh significantly. To know the contours of your living are a prototype for haunting must be demoralizing.

What does historical remorse do to one's moral lifeworld? How does one recover? What does *be*-ing in *this* kind of history do to someone?

What manner of woman does it take to remake history? To un-haunt? To de-terrorize? To usher in safety?

Truly understanding and fighting against the knowing that one is white and woman must be fracturing—the potential trapped by the problem.

No history is whole. Fracturing has happened and is happening everywhere.

I am watching to see what we do with this reality.

seven

Every observation has a history—has a story in friendship with white women embedded within.

In these experiences, the best that I have been able to conclude is that careful observation must happen.

For me, watching is part of friendship—a friendship loyal first and foremost to myself. Careful observation; the care is there for a reason. I care about myself enough to look out for myself, for the only one completely attuned to my life and the intricacies of my existence is me.

I am cognizant of tears and terror because they have tried desperately to shape how I imagine myself. I have had to talk myself off ledges of false accountability for hurting feelings that were in fact hauntings. But I am not responsible for feelings that do not even know themselves!

I will not mammy ghosts.

Tears that taint and (try to) bleed me are not my burden. I won't clean up messes I did not make.

I will, however, name the trappings. Whiteness is complicated. White womanhood is complicit. And the dangerous irony is that this brand of womanhood is overly expressive.

What it is trying to say, I am not sure.

I do not know if white women even know what they are trying to say outside of "*even I* have not sat down with the details of my body!"

It would take tremendous security and self-perception to fully take this truth in—let alone *want* to do something about it. Perhaps this is the most challenging observation: Do white women want to be *more than* white women?

What that'd entail, only white women will be able to discern. This is not my most pressing business. Reclaiming the virtue of tears is, however, for I need tears too.

eight

I refuse to let salt water be tainted for me. I come from a water people. My being knows salt water is too important to surrender to mishandling.

I know differently—that stains on clothing cull patterns that tell fruitful narratives. I know because they are in the clothes in which my mothers and fathers take deep pride. Our stain patterns are too elaborate to surrender to whiteness.

Stains do not have to bleed onto people, do not have to bleed people.

Stains can illuminate patterns that can say something. Remember, I watch people—my own included.

We wear in our skin divine messages of perseverance beyond the absurdity of this plane. And it is absurd to be a Black woman who is not hell-bent on first befriending herself. Whether white women catch up to this truth is an inquiry littered with white question marks.

Love towards oneself should never be the Black woman's question. If it is, it is only because the mission to separate us from knowing what we need has managed to gain a foothold. And sometimes footholds look like white women earnestly wanting to be on the right side of history by journeying alongside us.

We don't have time. Or space.

We must choose (Black) friendship—loving ourselves more than the idea of harmony. We must wisdom strategically, keeping our hearts and soul-health in the center of all we do and aspire to do.

We must never doubt our observations: that whiteness and womanhood have crafted a clever curse that has trapped its own beneficiaries.

But curses do not scare us.

Black women, *we* are divine beings. We have always known this. Their strange magic can invite terror, but our holiness is discerning, observing, counter-constructing pathways to health and peace for ourselves and those we love.

We love ourselves enough to know when to leave and when to wish well. We know how to stop the bleeding, how to detox and purify our presence.

We know when to leave and when to wish well.

Sometimes, white women have to be left to their own devices.

And broken devices are not our concern; we were not the ones who engineered their chaos.

We, instead, are founding our own mending.

We are too busy imparting divinity, planting our blessedness in souls who thirst—a divinity that sometimes blossoms from tears. But these tears do not flood, their stains do not ruin. They instead beautify, deify, and water the cosmos with a sage mixture of a maker's magic and sanctity.

Oluwa. My God—how holy are we?

10

Velynn's Response

Silencing Ghosts, Settling into Sisterhood

Velynn Brown

I know about tears that stain like blood-ghosts that hide behind human eyes. I've experienced the recklessness of whiteness in friendships. Friendships that felt like family—close-up, intimate, reliable—only to collapse in an unexpected blow. A blow that punched the heart and swung below the belt of dignity, decency, and devotion. A blow that knocked out all hope of a comeback.

My Sis Tomi's laser observations and cautiously loving warnings, of both the complex power white women hold and the carelessness in which many carry it, hit me square in the heart.

No chaser.

No filter.

No fluff.

And for this Black woman, whose prerequisite in surviving while Black in the Pacific Northwest meant learning how to skate around white women's tears like invisible land mines, her words were almost too much truth.

Too close.

Too real.

Too much truth.

But isn't truth the thing that we need? Isn't truth the thing that sets us free? While it can be easier to ignore the things that have harmed us, easy to give only a nod to that dull but deep pain that only comes up once in a while, truth also holds the possibility of saving our lives. The transparent exposure of calling to light what is ill, harmful, ugly, dangerous—like a cancer diagnosis we know—saves lives. Racism is a disease. Racism has caused *dis*-ease to my body and chronic trauma to my life. Racism, like cancer, untreated is killing us. How, you might ask?

It is because racism is baked into every institution, leaving Black people—especially Black girls and women—susceptible to maltreatment, discrimination, and neglect. Systemic and cultural racism brings both internal and external stressors that feed upon weakened immune systems, generational poverty, and insufficient medical treatments. Researchers have long documented that Black people have higher rates of heart disease, asthma, and obesity, along with many other illnesses. Black people's genes are not deadly. Rather, the way America has organized itself is deadly to the Black body, and this is what Tomi is calling us honestly to see in the light.

The way America has organized itself is deadly to the Black body.

Let me say again—for the people in the back—the way America has organized itself is deadly to the Black body.

Meaning, in this country, white women will always be the first and saved in this racial hierarchical line. Out of survival, I have been conditioned to ignore the disease of racism in my body. I've been asked to ignore the hemorrhaging of my own pain to wipe up white women's tears with napkins of niceness and tissues of "that's ok's." All while being sliced and diced by knives of humiliation, horror, and manipulated helplessness. Over time, the invisible slashes of micro- and macro-aggressions in my relationship with white people—especially white women—have left me exhausted, sick, and fearful.

It is deeply disturbing that something as sacred as tears can be used as weapons to spear the dignity and humanity of my people. Where I'm from, tears release thunderous joy and oftentimes stand as the sole witness to that sneak attack. Where I'm from, tears wash down like holy water on foreheads and cheeks to relieve the incomprehension of premature murders and lynchings. In my eyes, Black women's tears are sacred.

However, tears dropped by Black women in public do not get the same response. Black women's tears are questionable, emotional, just water in the eyes. But when a white woman cries, the whole world stops and takes notice. Nobody is safe—especially a Black body—when white women cry.

As Tomi so eloquently unpacks, cry-shaming is a skill white women have mastered that takes the focus off of the one being targeted to fully display the female oppressor's "assumed assault." The Carolyn Bryants that kill our Emmett Tills. The Amy Coopers who call 911, hijacking the peace and tranquility of just trying to watch the beauty of a bird's life. The "Karens" that bully and pounce and arrest our everyday rhythms and simple delights of life are always among us.

In my experience, Karens have full monopoly and autonomy to lash out their projected fears or reign in their assumed privileges wherever and whenever they please. However, when Black women cry out for help, we are killed instead of saved. Since 2015 police have fatally shot nearly 250 Black women. Eighty-nine of these women, like Breonna Taylor, were killed in their homes or residences where they often stayed.[1]

Not even three hours from leaving Collegeville with Tomi and our new *We Deserve to Heal* Sistah-tribe, I encountered my newest interaction with a Karen in the wild. Filled to the brim with so much Black woman sisterhood, joy, and love, I was aware but not burdened by being once again "the only" Black person in the one-hundred-and-thirty-eight-seater Alaska Airlines aircraft. I was determined to hold on to all the Black Girl Magic I could hold upon my return home.

As I was nestling into my airline seat, I was so grateful for the smiling, nice-ish hipster young white male and the empty seat between us. I was equally appreciative of the window seat that gave me my picture-perfect moment. Raising my window shade to catch the mid-morning skies of Minnesota, I heard a forceful southern drawl that seemed to own the plane. Noticing that the voice was not attached to a Black- or browned-skinned body, my heart began to race. Admittedly when a southern accent is attached to someone who looks like me, I feel safe, at home. My grandmother Cecil Mae, of Minden, Arkansas, descent, held her southern inflections all the way to her centennial years on this earth. But when a white person from the same Southern region raises her voice to a Black-skinned body, it is not always favorable. In my personal experiences, it has not fared well. I was triggered—stomach tight, body tensed, ears perked.

"Close that window! Don't leave that window up."

My heart felt like it had just gotten stung by a bee. My hand froze on the tiny airline shade, leaving the window a third of the way open.

"Hey!" A voice coming from across my aisle spoke again. "I said, 'close that window!'"

My head turned to look in the direction of the voice that was spewing out like lava. The loud, agitated voice I could now locate was attached to a gray-haired, white, feeble-framed body. Her eyes were trying to pierce through me, maybe even split through me. That unspoken rage running under her wrinkled eyes felt all too familiar. It was not flesh; what I saw was spiritual. The ghost of racist past is what it was, and every bloodline of my ancestral lineage was beating through my body and standing at full attention.

Without even thinking about how to respond, my finger went up high, straight up in the air. Not the middle one. My momma raised me right. It was my index finger. The finger that we raise in church to pardon ourselves out of the sanctuary when service is in order. Usually, this sign is directed to the usher on post as a gesture of respect rather than an apology for doing something wrong. Is it wrong to excuse yourself to the Ladies Room? Was it wrong for me to have to excuse myself for opening the shade to the window of my own paid seat?

It was not wrong.

I had done nothing wrong.

Yet, somehow, her discomfort with my ease, access, and agency to do what I wanted to do in my own seat, for just ten seconds, was too much. My Black liberation, as "the only" on the plane, was too much for her. My joy of capturing the moment and the memories I wanted to possess as my own was a threat to her.

With my left church finger still in the air, I placed my phone down on my lap with only my right hand. I then touched the camera icon with my right index finger. Took a deep breath and continued to take my picture of the mid-morning Minnesota horizon. I then closed my blind and pretended all that had just transpired was just a bad dream.

In these streets—or should I say in these planes—you have to have a supernatural imagination to keep your joy as a Black woman.

Throughout the entire flight, I never returned my gaze back to her direction. I was taught at a very young age to ignore stewing white people. Even if you have not done anything wrong. Especially if you are right and they are still brewing. Especially when they are particularly interested in you. Get small, get quiet, don't make a sound.

But she continued to have a conversation with me.

"Oh look at her."
"She's just going to open that window up anyway."

Why was she so fixated on me?

I wasn't sure if, at this moment, this woman was even aware that she was or whose she was. But I was. She continued to observe me—like an animal caged for her joy and entertainment. It was just a bodily reaction, like a stretch or a yawn to be focused on me for a while. Tomi talked about wondering if white women even knew what they possessed, if they knew the substance of themselves. And all the while, white women get all the time in the world, in the movement, in the ministry, in this justice work to choose what they want to say and how they want to be.

We don't.

I don't.

I don't get to take my time, take up the tears. And by no means do I get to afford to be unaware.

In this moment, I was very aware.

I was aware of how many rows of people were now quiet observers of an offense I somehow committed by opening my window. I was aware of the speed of my heart rate. Even with all of the deep breaths I was intentionally practicing, I wondered how many days would this take off my life. Right at that moment a group text with a picture attached popped up on my phone.

I clicked the message, and the most beautiful picture of all my Sistahs came through. Water beaded around the corner of my eyes and a warm shower washed over my heart. I let my tears fall. Tears of joy, healing, and belonging—not terror. Tears that held healing, calm, and balm to my soul. This is the usefulness and ministry of tears. I took a long deep breath and closed my eyes. Instantly I was teleported back into the presence, care, and covering of my *We Deserve to Heal* sanctuary of sisterhood. Even though I wasn't in the picture with them because my flight was the first, seeing them all stare back was all I needed in that moment to be held, to be witnessed. I was not alone; their sisterhood settled me. Their reflection was a reminder to me of the Black Girl Magic tribe I am a part of, giving me a moment in real time to ground myself and adjust my crown.

My heart settled back down and so did the old lady. I found my happy spot which faithfully consists of my favorite pen, journal, brown-sugared green Matcha, and my AirPods. I must have dozed off a bit because the next thing I heard was, "We will be landing at our final destination of Portland, Oregon, in just ten more minutes."

Thrilled to be home, I had almost forgotten about the incident until I could feel those eyes pulsing at me. My neighbor was quick to hop out his seat and down the aisle. Surely he may have felt the heat of her darted focus on me. He had been caught in the middle of this minor racial battle, and he seemed quick not to get caught in any more crossfires.

Out of respect, I unconsciously waited for the elderly white lady to walk down the aisle first. Why was I being so nice to her? Maybe I had overreacted? Maybe I was overthinking or being too sensitive?

She was still trying to get up with her cane as I paused to let her go ahead of me. I still refused to look her in the eyes. And then I heard it again, that poking, controlling, you-better-stay-in-your-place-negro, white-ghost voice again.

"You alright, Girl? What's wrong with you? You'll be alright."

I stopped and took in another long breath.

Her words hung in the air how winter's first icicles hang on trees—suspended, appearing to be held up by themselves but attached to limbs. This woman was attached to something bigger than what I could see with my eye.

She chuckled to herself and to the frozen witnesses stacked up waiting behind that I also chose to look at instead of her. I was not going to let his darkness have its way.

Once again, I had not made this all up in my head. Once again, my dignity, peace, and freedom would be up for the taking—if I let it. But this was a spiritual battle, and I refused to continue to be a puppet of the evil one's ploys to still my light, my breath, my life.

In that same moment there was so much my inner Black-Girl-clap-back-self wanted to rise up and say. But that day wasn't worth it. Honestly it gave me more satisfaction knowing I only gave her one minute of my attention rather than a whole airplane ride of irritation and control she was wanting to prey on.

Some days the ghosts are big.
Some days they are smaller.
Sometimes I have energy to fight.
Sometimes I have nothing at all.
This is where I have the power and the control.
I get to choose my response.
This day I also realized I was truly not alone.

Tomi's transparent observations and loving warning to Black women not only affirmed our experiences with white women, it also justified our freedom as Black women to no longer tolerate these attacks, to no longer silence our experiences nor internalize the poison of white tears, ghosts, and traumas. Her strength makes me stronger.

We have drowned in oceans of white women's tears. Our backs are weary of the lash and their labor. We no longer have to entertain the fragility, guilt, or shame of white women's fears. It's not an issue of exclusion. No, it is a matter of life and death. My life is worth saving first. Period. Enough of my life has been taken away.

We don't have to look into the eyes of our oppressors. We can stare down the demons while holding on to our light. We can instead be seen, loved, and filled up by our sisters. Instead of curses, y'all, it is time for blessings.

For every ghost may there be an ancestor
For every tear may there be oceans of joy and laughter
For every Karen may there be circles, sights, and divine appointments with your found sacred Sister tribes
For every spiritual battle may there be long years filled with ease, rest, and divine imagination
For every truth you receive may you be brave enough to receive true freedom, healing, and restoration

Note

1. Jennifer Jenkins Marisa Iati, "Nearly 250 Women Have Been Fatally Shot by Police since 2015," *The Washington Post*, September 4, 2020, https://www.washingtonpost.com/graphics/2020/investigations/police-shootings-women/.

11

Finding My Way

Paula Owens Parker

My ancestral roots on this side of the Atlantic are in Norfolk County (now Chesapeake) and Princess Anne County (now Virginia Beach), Virginia. DNA identifies my ancestral home somewhere in what is now Ghana and Nigeria. My father's ancestors were enslaved, and my mother's ancestors were free. My father was a dentist and a civil rights leader in our hometown. My mother was a teacher. My family's essential values were education, family history, faith, and service to the community.

My world was segregated from kindergarten through college. Watching my family navigate white folks and racism, I knew better than to let white folks get too close. I separated my social and family life from my work life. I did not have direct relationships with white women until after I graduated from college and was hired by a large international corporation in upstate New York.

I felt like an immigrant in a foreign land, a world where my parents did not know the language, the culture, or the politics. I had to find my own way. And on top of that, the times were changing; the Black Power movement, feminist movement, sexual revolution, Vietnam protests, and Harlem Cultural Festival were in full swing. To insulate myself, I sought out Black coworkers to help me navigate this strange new world. I was wary of white women because of the behavior I saw on television toward Black children seeking an education. Their snarls and screams still ring in my ears when I get triggered by "Central Park Karen" calling the police on a Black man who was birdwatching and "Becky," the privileged, sheltered, mean white girl who manipulates to get her way.

When I moved back to Virginia, corporate America was more recognizable; they were Plantation 2.0. "Miss Anne" was alive and well as a supervisor and secretary. These circumstances intensified my effort to find my own way. With the blueprint of my upbringing, I began my spiritual quest for meaning and purpose in my life. There had to be more to life than the daily grind of corporate America.

A perpetual seeker of knowledge, I read, attended conferences, and ultimately signed up for a training class for lay counselors. I did not know the material would trigger my own trauma. At the end of the course, my instructor recommended that I meet with two women in the class. They were part of a newly emerging healing prayer ministry at their church. I spoke with them briefly, and they agreed to meet with me. We made an appointment.

Because it was a weekday morning, the church was empty. The room where we met was one of their Sunday school classrooms. There was a blackboard at one end of the room and a small rectangular conference table in the center. Extra chairs lined up against the blank beige walls. The room had no windows, and the ceiling light made it feel like an office.

Jane sat at one end and Shirley at the other; these two white women invited me to sit at the table between them. Both of them had their Bibles. I came with nothing, and when I sat down, I told them that if this experience didn't answer my questions, I would give up trying to discern what I was supposed to believe and do. It was too complicated and confusing. I had too many unanswered questions.

We could not have had a more diverse demographic. Jane was the wife of a physician from a very wealthy family, and Shirley was the wife of a Pittsburgh factory worker and daughter of a hairdresser. Jane was in her early sixties, Shirley was in her mid-fifties, and I was forty. We were mothers. Jane and I were college-educated, and Shirley was a high school graduate. Jane and her husband were separated, and Shirley and I were married. Except in a setting like this, where all three of us sought a deeper spiritual life and vocation, our paths would have never crossed.

Over the next ten months, these women created liminal space for the Spirit to heal my conscious and unconscious traumatic memories. They listened, prayed, and carefully held me when painful memories seared and unconditional love overflowed. Their nurturing and sincere presence opened me to be healed from old wounds and make way for new beginnings.

All the weekly sessions were not deep, heavy, and profound; there was a particular session that was light with laughter when we connected as women who had, despite race, age, and class, found common ground and witnessed the *imago dei* in each other, the Christ within. We validated each other with that "I know what you mean" nod. For a moment, race became secondary in my search for health and wholeness.

We created an authentic relationship because we entered the relationship intentionally, allowing the Spirit to be present to navigate our interactions.

But what they offered was not enough. It was healing and empowering, but for what? What was the endgame here? What was I supposed to do?

The answer became apparent when I participated in a healing service at their church. Prayer and praise opened the service, then the guest preacher gave his message and invited people to come forward for prayer. When he gently touched my forehead, I felt like I floated to the floor. I was aware of Jane and Shirley praying over me and the music in the background. I don't know how long I was on the floor, but when I got up, I was in tears, not of pain but joy! It was joy unspeakable. At that moment, I knew my life's purpose: to be part of the healing ministry and create opportunities for others to recognize and be free of old trauma. My experience with Jane and Shirley set the tone and direction for my life and ministry. It was enough to find my way to seminary, ordination, and further training.

Jane and Shirley were not the only white women to leave an imprint on my life. I was one of three Black people who attended the training where I met Sandi. The classroom, which held about forty people, was packed. There was standing room only. Everyone gave her their undivided attention as she lectured on generational healing and described behavioral, emotional, and physical patterns of inherited trauma. Like me, they had never heard anything like this before. Standing in line after the lecture, you could sense Sandi's energy and passion in her animated response to our questions. After she and her husband relocated to Virginia, we became ministry partners. Over the years, we developed classes, curricula, and programs. We organized healing conferences and retreats. Our presence together made a statement as we created spiritual sanctuaries for people to heal. However, for me, it was not enough.

My training used Western European methodology and theology. It focused on the individual and, at best, the family through generational healing. There was no focus on healing the community. As a Black woman, the trauma of racism, sexism, and classism in the Black community was obvious; the white women I encountered were in denial. That truth was the elephant in the room. However, I felt it wasn't the time to take on these issues because it would have derailed our relationship, which was integral in setting the trajectory and tone of my ministry.

Despite Jane, Shirley, and Sandi's lack of awareness about these traumas, I still had positive, healing interactions with them. In contrast, I have had challenging encounters with white women coworkers who stifle opportunities by manipulating rules to exclude me. They ask for my expertise and then try to insert themselves into the project for which they are not qualified nor have the resources. They ignore my suggestions and then make it seem like it was their idea. They nitpick to harass so they will feel less threatened. They deny or minimize my life experiences. They turn on the tears when they can't get their way. They try to invade my space because they are drawn to, but can't have, Black Girl Magic.

I became adept at reading faces and body language, listening for cues and dog whistles, and the essential code-switching skill. Strategically navigating the racial landscape is wearying. Being intentional about family and cultural history keeps me rooted and grounded. It reduces the opportunity to be manipulated and deceived. Self-care and self-awareness are a must. My Black girlfriends and I share our stories, our families, and our experiences without having to explain. With different interests, skills, and expertise, we complement and intersect as Black women. Racism, sexism, classism, social justice, politics, Black history, and advocacy are part of our ongoing conversation. But they are not my ministry partners.

I knew having my lived experience and perspective recognized and valued was paramount. Creating agency for myself and my community was crucial. I had to figure out a way to make that happen.

Even with clarity of purpose, I understood this is not a perfect world of peace and harmony. Not everyone wants to take the risk of being vulnerable. Not everyone understands or discerns that a deeper spiritual connection is feasible. Trauma, conflicting theologies, and limited exposure to "the Other" are only a few roadblocks. Silos and parallel universes exist.

As a Black woman, I had to make a way out of no way and create what I needed. So, I enrolled in a program providing the structure and accountability I needed and an advisor to guide me through the process.

I did not know what to expect when I walked into Dr. Katie Geneva Cannon's office. I wanted a Black woman as an advisor because the project was about generational healing in the African American community. I knew she would meet the requirements of my project committee. I'd met her before at events she sponsored. I knew who she was but did not "know" who she was.

Dressed in a purple and green African print dress, this beautiful brown-skinned woman with mixed grey natural hair, silver earrings, and colorful bracelets on both wrists greeted me with a warm smile. She pointed me to a chair opposite hers in front of one of two desks in her office, one where she did her "work" and the other where she sat with her students. Shelves full of books flanked both desks. The two file cabinets I found out later held former students' theses and dissertations. Pictures of former students, their families, and her nieces and nephews were taped to the shelves' edges, along with photos of her with Alice Walker, Cornel West, and James Cone. Awards and plaques were on the walls and top of the bookshelves. A red, black, and green afghan was draped on the black sofa near her office door. A map of Africa hung above it. There was a large painting of Zora Neale Hurston on the wall to the left of her "work" desk. Dr. Cannon said early in her career, when she traveled to events where she knew she would be the only Black person, she would take Zora with her for company. Zora was her muse.

I focused on getting work done without wasting her precious time, so I was surprised when she started the conversation, "How are you? Tell me about yourself and your family." She always started our weekly two-hour meetings with "How are you?" And she remembered my story and even asked me about things I had forgotten.

In one of our earlier meetings, she complimented me, and I mumbled under my breath, "You are just saying that." She looked at me with piercing eyes and said with a deadpan face, "I would not say it if I did not mean it." From that point on, I accepted her compliments and believed them.

I was always careful to respect her and her time. Still, somewhere along the way, she stopped being "The Reverend Dr. Katie Geneva Cannon," creator of an entirely new branch of theology named womanist theology, creator of the Center for Womanist Leadership, who knew all the academic celebrities and many others, who casually mentioned attending Toni Morrison's eightieth birthday party and flying to New York to join James Cone to support a Ph.D. student's defense over the weekend, and became just Katie.

It might have been the night I was home at my computer struggling with a problematic part of the project and lost in the proverbial "rabbit hole" when I heard my phone ring. She called to check on me. I was stunned. How did she know? Or, it might have been when she shared her pain and grief of losing her best friend to cancer. Or, it might have been when we got ice cream, laughed, and joked after she finished her presentation at Princeton. Or, it might have been her graciousness and accessibility. Or, her comedic sense of humor. Somewhere along the way, she became "Katie," so from this point on in this essay, I will call her Katie.

One of my favorite textbooks is *African American Female Mysticism: Nineteenth-Century Religious Activism* by Joy Bostic. The first two sentences in the first chapter made me put the book down and pace the floor. Bostic writes, "The religious quest for African American women is fundamentally a search for space and place. These movements involve the work of constructing emancipatory identities in the face of gender and racial stereotypes."[1] OMG! She nailed it! That is what I was searching for, my space and place. Something Jane, Shirley, and Sandi could never help me find.

Katie and her Black women classmates in their Ph.D. program tried to align themselves with the Black male students. They were rejected because they were women. When they tried to align with the white female students, they were not welcomed because they were Black.

In response to the racist and sexist rebuff, Katie constructed womanist theology as her emancipatory identity. A space and place for Black women's lived experiences to be recognized, affirmed, and celebrated. She created a space and place for Black women in the church, academy, and community, in all walks of life, with all their gifts and graces.

Katie helped me create that emancipatory space for my work. She gave me the tools to integrate my Black womanist self into the white world in a way that both Black and white could see me for who I was: a Black woman who cared deeply about healing and firmly believed the Spirit can and will connect and transform differences if you are open to her. Katie taught me how to bridge the cultural and racial gap and make divine connections. Katie showed me the way to myself.

Jane and Shirley were integral to my discovering my vocation. Sandi was key in implementing it. But they could not take me where they had never been. Reflecting on my relationships with them, I realize opportunities can present themselves under unorthodox circumstances and with people I would never consider to have anything in common.

I learned that if I am willing to take risks, walk into rooms with people I don't know, and let the Spirit guide me into mystical spaces, my walls will come down, my perspectives will change, empathy will emerge, and my eyes will open to see with clearer vision and forever eyes.

Note

1. Joy R. Bostic, "African American Female Mysticism: The Nineteenth Century Contextual Landscape," in *African American Female Mysticism: Nineteenth-Century Religious Activism* (Palgrave Macmillan, 2013), 1.

12

Kadeisha's Response

A Hairstory of Finding My Way

Kadeisha M. Bonsu

For my mama, my aunties, and all the women who loved, formed, and styled me.

I never had white friends. I had friends. I never had Black friends. I had friends. My first direct relationships with white people were in preschool. I had many, many friends who were white because during that time, I lived in a predominantly white town. I went to school with white people, but I came home to my people. Growing up in Union, New Jersey, gave me access to excellent schools and resources. My first noticing of race was that in elementary school it seemed that the majority of white kids walked to school with their parents, and all the Black kids were being bused in from Vauxhall, the neighboring town with a different zip code, its own library branch, and its own post office, but still considered to be a part of the Town of Union. Vauxhall was, in essence, the Black side of town. I will never forget one of my white classmates telling me that he was scared to come to Central Five—the singular grade school for all fifth graders in Union, but located on the Vauxhall side of town. He shared that he was afraid he would get shot. I remember knowing even in that moment, at eleven years old, that this was a harmfully racist projection. I'd probably even gotten defensive and told him off, as the little Jersey girl in me learned to do when someone needed to be checked. The funny thing is I'd never heard or seen a gun before, and I'd never imagined getting shot walking and playing in my neighborhood. It was a far-fetched idea to me and deviated from my perceived and actual reality. I had to resist his imagination and stick to what I knew to be true.

During my time in elementary school, I met my first best friend, a white girl named Stephanie V. We shared the same first grade classroom, and we had the best of times together. Stephanie moved away a year after we made acquaintance, and I knew then that I would miss her. Somewhere in the midst of grieving my friend moving away, I forgot her last name. There would be many times later on, at the dawn of the internet and social media, that I'd think, "If only I could remember her last name." I'd wonder, "Where is she, what does she look like, what is her life like, and . . . would she remember me?" When I think of her, I think of the Lisa Frank products we enjoyed reveling in amid the art and wonder of Washington Elementary School.

I've spent years trying to remember Stephanie V.'s last name. I loved her. We had fun together. The one, and only, time I questioned our differences was when it was her turn to come to our side of town, the Black side. I'd suddenly become conscious that my world was different than what I knew of hers, and I was about to invite her into that. My mother and her mother spoke by phone, and they were both okay with her coming over. I was excited, but I'm sure even my mother was nervous as she told me that week, "You all need to clean up before your friend comes over." But it wasn't a typical "clean your room" admonishment that most parents have to remind their children of. It was a fringe of her own anxiety peeking through and surveying the nooks and crannies of our home. Much like someone may try to baby-proof a house, she was company-proofing the house, but I know now and she knew then that it wasn't just any company-proofing—it was white gaze company-proofing.

I had been on a play date to Stephanie's house in Union, and, surprisingly, I'd never hung out in that neighborhood surrounding our esteemed elementary school. So, what an exciting moment it was to go *inside* one of those houses. Our messy house was full of people, full of joy and life. It was different than what I saw in her house. Our blended family was by no means traditional. We rented our home, and my mom would say, "We lived in it." It was not for show. Stephanie's home was beautiful, and they owned their home. Now, from my adult lens, I can realize that I *assumed* "The V's" owned their home and that this was not something most Black people could do, but all white people could do. I assumed that. Of course, I now know that not to be true, but I believe my then-child mind was working out the noticings of race and class. Stephanie's family had the purported "American Dream," as she shared a home with her mom, dad, and older sister. I would never live in a house with my mom *and* dad, and how would I explain our complicated family dynamic that seemed so outside the world of white people—or at least the middle-class white people I encountered on the school playground.

As a kid, I longed for aspects of this fantasy American Dream. I imagined whiteness and my assimilation to it to be the ticket to the Dream. I slipped from my reality into my imagination of an alternative world. I couldn't completely ignore this imagination because it was starkly different from my reality. Perhaps, like my fifth-grade classmate who was terrified of being shot on the Black side of town, I had my own imaginations. Unlike his, my imagination was marked with beauty and the fantasy of a lovely escape; his was marked with darkness and despair of slipping from this life harmed at the hands of a Black person. (Sadly, sometimes little white boys grow up to be grown white men who play out the fears of their childhood imaginations, manifested by a need to protect themselves against the imagined fear of a Black boy carrying a brush in his pocket that they perceive to be the gun that could have shot them when they were little and attending school on the Black side of town.)

My fantasies included things like looking like the white women I'd seen around me. At one point, I'd even wondered what I would look like if my skin was fair or I was light skinned. I didn't imagine what it would look like if it was white or a bit more on the paler side of fair, mostly because I actually loved being a little Black girl, and at home, my Blackness was affirmed without hesitation. I was surrounded by beautiful dark-skinned Black women. My sister was light skinned and equally as beautiful. My mom called us "salt and pepper"—certainly influenced by the hip hop group. I didn't want to *be* white, but I wanted to know what *my* world would be like and how *my* beauty *might* be "enhanced" if I had some of the features white girls had like long flowing hair.

It was during gatherings in the school auditorium that I'd be most likely to slip into this fantasy world. There in that auditorium, we'd gather each afternoon. From that auditorium, they would call our bus numbers, or someone's parents would appear at the opposite exit for pick up. There was plenty of time for people watching while we waited for our respective chauffeurs to pick us up and take us home, whether by escorted walk, car, or bus—though we already knew who was taking the bus and who was not. People watching can be fun, but as a little girl, it caused me to become conscious of difference and tempted toward conformity. I'd people-watch. I'd look at the adults and the kids in the room. I'd watch the grown-ups, those with the power—mostly white women teachers and staff. And because representation did not matter in the '90s white suburbs, sometimes, I'd see the cultural beauty standards of whiteness even further projected when we would have school assemblies. We would be entertained by puppeteers, magic shows, plays, musical guests, and more—all white. I don't remember seeing people who looked like me on that school stage. The only time we'd see us on the stage was when it was actually us. I didn't want to be white, but I did envy their hair at times. Their hair was long, hanging down their back or at least to their shoulders. Their hair swung like my Barbie dolls', even the brown Barbie dolls that had not yet evolved into Barbies with afros and 4a, b, and c textures. Their hair was long and straight. Mine was not. Their hair never puffed up. Without the assistance of a perm, mine did. We retired the pressing comb by the time I'd gotten to kindergarten, trading it for a relaxer. No amount of *Just for Me* made my hair as swingy and long as theirs, nor as fine and straight. Still, after a long, hard day of play, my hair just stuck up, peaking out of my bobos and barrettes. It did not hang down or swing low like Stephanie's did after a long, hard day of play.

Putting my pink raincoat atop my head, I pretended my hair could swing, long and flowing down my back. That's when I started trying to blend into the world of the white girls and women around me. Putting the neck of the shirt around the perimeter of my Black curly baby hair and styling it by wrapping a hair tie around the shirt, is one of the earliest instances I can remember attempting to conform to dominant culture beauty standards. But thankfully, when I went home, I was surrounded by fierce Black women who were skilled in the art and beauty of Black hair. Like Paula, I found a refuge among my people when the spaces that nurtured me, like school, could not ultimately keep and sustain me. Around my family, I found sanctuary. My aunties were cosmetologists, and they coifed the most beautiful styles that allowed me to love and embrace the versatility of Black hair. Later into my hair journey, beyond the virgin relaxer stage, I would learn from my beautician aunts something startling: We used perms to relax—aka straighten—our hair, but white people used perms to curl their hair. "Go figure!" This was mind boggling. "I wanted their hair, but they wanted mine? Hmmm." It would be little moments of education like this that would break me out of my white imagination and reinsert me into reality, bringing me to the beginnings of consciousness and embrace of my Blackness. All those years in elementary school, I'd believed that white was right. But among those beauty shop conversations, I'd hear one of my aunts exclaim from time to time, "Who said white was right?!" We would all crack up. Though a lighthearted moment, it invited me to be Black and Proud. Like Paula, finding spiritual refuge and safety in the warmth of her mentor and friend's presence, I found refuge, safety, and warmth from the weary world of immersion in whiteness day in and day out by sitting in my mama's kitchen for a day of washing, drying, and styling—and sometimes enjoying the chatter, buzz, and smell of hair spray and curling irons in my aunts' hair salons, Hair-I-Am and Studio-B.

I would never have imagined that those moments of enduring and then learning to enjoy our weekend hairstyling sessions in preparation for the school week would be the thread that would carry me into my authenticity as an adolescent through emerging adult and into my womanhood. I found my way through my hair. I shed the weight of white beauty standards and traveled to worlds that reminded me that Black hair is bold, beautiful, creative, resilient, proud, loud, splendid, majestic—the list goes on. Black hair is as glimmerous as the Blue Magic grease my mom greased my scalp with after plaiting it tightly into neatly styled cornrows. Black hair is dark and slick like the black *Pro Styl* gel we used to smooth those curls into an updo and then slip the edges into the fineness of baby hair with a toothbrush repurposed for hairstyling. Learning to love and enjoy my Black hair just as it was saved me from whiteness and transported me deeper into my own true expression. College would be the time when my hair adventures winded more deeply down the joyful roads of play and exploration.

I could wear it cut low, I could wear it in a big fro, I could wear it straight, or I could let it flow in long braids. I could change its color. I could change its texture. But best of all, I could embrace its wonder and let the world behold the beauty of me, even as I traversed the quads of the predominantly white, gothic, Southern Ivy wonderland that shifted my home from my small Black community to a world more white than I'd ever seen. By the time I got to graduate school, I was already at home with my expression of myself in the world through fashion and hair. But I owe much of this journey of finding my way to sitting in the seats of the kitchen beauticians that formed and shaped me. My mom, my aunts, my cousins. Beautiful Black women, immersed, conformed, and affirmed by the trends and cultural beauty standards they helped create as hair artists, and they displayed with confidence as caring adults in my life. They created a world of home that I could return to when white people, institutions, and structures wearied me. They washed my hair and rolled it. They dried it, wrapped and pinned it. Because of them, I could shake loose my doobie, and return to the big world that may not have been made with me in mind, but I had found my way. And with the confidence of my crown, I'd pave ways forward so that my little girl, with her little baby puffs and ribbons, and my little boy, with his neatly coiled locs, could one day find their way too. My hairstory is the golden brick road to the way I've found amid the perils of whiteness. My hairstory gives light to the promises ascertained through our confidence that dusted off and broke loose from demonic imaginations insisting that our realities weren't good enough. My Blackness can be loud. It can be soft. But whatever it may be, I am the me I am despite the perils and because of the resilience of the promises.

A Promise for the Descendent Daughters:
They call us Black, God calls us *lovely*.
They call us bitter like grinds of coffee,
But the folk call us *sweeter* like the blackest *berry*.
May our *crowns* be our LIBERATION,
"[O] daughters of Jerusalem, I'm dark and lovely
like the tents of Kedar,
like the curtains of Solomon."[1]
O, Black women,
We are *Dark and Lovely*,
no lye.

Note

1. *Holy Bible, International Standard Version* (Davidson Press LLC, 1995), Song of Solomon 1:5.

13

The So-Called Life of Belonging

Discovering the Concept of Friendship through a Historical Lens

QUANTRILLA ARD

I remember her in my mind and in my heart as one of my very first friends. Her blonde, almost white hair framed her face. Her wide-set, dreamy eyes were the color of clear Mediterranean water, and she had a perfectly pink pout. Even as a child, I knew that she was as sweet and beautiful inside as she was out. We gravitated toward each other naturally as any two children would—or should, as I think back on that time. We were both students in the same first-grade class, and I was the only little Black girl. She saw me. She would place her little hand in mine as we walked to the playground during recess or wave me over to the lunch table and make space for me to sit next to her. In what felt like an ocean of eyes observing our interactions, she saw me by being present in friendship with me—in stark contrast to treatment by other classmates.

Multiple school changes weakened the bond of our friendship. The final blow was dealt during a conversation we had on the side of the school building. It was a bright and warm day, and the rays of the sun highlighted my face and warmed my body, but the light and warmth didn't reach my heart. It was the day she told me she was moving away and would not be coming back to our school. *Our school*, the place where our connection had been established and taken root. That same year, I recall hearing another girl in the class mention (not subtly either) that she couldn't play with me anymore anyways because her mom had said so. This was the first of several heartaches in my friendships with white girls. I didn't even think to consider how these heartaches would or could affect me as an adult.

Middle school didn't change the dynamics much, but it definitely changed the players. There were distinct shifts in my experiences with preteen and teenage white girls. These shifts ranged from friendly (but not a friend) to downright despicable. Bullying was a pervasive part of my experience. This included comments about everything, especially my appearance: I was too dark-skinned (but not too "Black" as that is an important distinction here); my glasses were too thick; I sounded "white"; I was too curvy. There was also the weirdness that despite the bullying, people still liked me. My teachers praised my work, and I was often asked to represent my class and the school at various outings. This enraged them to taunt me even more. It was a gnarly, tangled mess out of which I wanted to be delivered. But it was school. How does a child-turned-young-woman find freedom in a space she is mandated to be in five days a week, ten months of the year?

There was another friend, quite different from the first. Darker features, equally as lovely. She was my freedom exactly when I needed it as sixth, seventh, and eighth grades were a mixed bag of hormones and hot mess expresses. Yet, I felt permission to be. She wasn't the most popular. She didn't have love letters being passed her way during English, but she was fierce and stubborn with a fire in her amber eyes. I was drawn to her carefree laugh and tough exterior, but there was a sweetness she reserved for me, her friend who helped her navigate family trauma just by being present with a listening ear. Again, distance, time, and relocation stole what had been a grounding friendship for me during those awkward years of puberty.

I left this predominantly white, Protestant upbringing after eighth-grade graduation only to find myself in another similar environment, but let's make it a boarding school for fun. Only it was a breeding ground for diminishing self-confidence because you lived with the characters in your story 24/7. Those two years passed quickly with barely a blur, but there was a seed that had been planted that I wouldn't see the fruit of until years later. Self-confidence is a critical indicator of relationships—and not just platonic ones. What I didn't realize then was that this diminishing would have weight in those nonplatonic relationships as well, leaving the door of love ajar yet hanging on hinges that weren't able to bear its weight.

Coming of age as a Black girl in white spaces was hard. My mother was a very large part of the resilience I developed, and it wasn't without the undoing of my self-hate. She did her best to remind me of my beauty from the unique name she passed down to the velvety hue of my skin. But those were the very targets of my foes. It was hard for me to accept who I was as friendships with white girls failed and I carried the jeers of others who acted as if my very presence was an inconvenience. Leaving this glossy world made a huge difference. I was adamant that my next experience would be full to the brim of Black everything. I was HBCU bound, and I wanted to feel all the connections to my kinfolk, my skin-folk. Professors, roommates, boyfriends, besties, all of it. I needed the change from all white everything. I enjoyed the change, but I noticed that there was still something quite off about my time in college. This feeling of other-ness persisted even though I was surrounded by people who looked and believed like me. There was a level of expectation I had from this community. A redemption of sorts to bring me peace and resolution to what I couldn't understand in the majority white space. Although my time there was cathartic in many ways, some of the old feelings resurfaced. I learned that proximity to whiteness and anti-Blackness exist in multiple spaces—not just the typical ones. And in this fertile soil, the seeds of diminished self-confidence took root and grew strange fruit.

Similar to growing up with and residing in boarding school with white girls who were either indifferent or insidious, there was also a faction of Black girls who stoked the fires of hatred or dismissal. They existed in suburban Florida where I grew up. Also, in Georgia where I spent my last two years in high school. And lastly, they showed up again in a small agricultural town in Alabama where I navigated undergrad. In my youth, these Black girls were tools wielded in the hands of white girls who didn't want the bruises their actions caused to come from their blows, but their participation in my misery created just as much damage. These marionettes would do and say harmful things such as calling me "darkie" or "blackie" or start conversations about how ugly I was because of my skin tone. They would comment on how large my breasts or backside were and how no one thought I was pretty. They would huddle in a group and giggle saying I couldn't possibly have looked in a mirror before leaving home and "show up" in public like this. This same spirit possessed many a Black girl who was "grown-*ish*," walking the halls of my major department and the dormitories in which I lived, and who marched across the stage *cum laude* taking selfies on disposable cameras.

Friendship has always played out in a different manner for me. Even now, I often wonder if my friendships would be different under other circumstances. I am an only child, and I must share the significance of that along with the racialized messages I received about friendship and belonging. I am the oldest cousin on my maternal side of the family, and I lived several states away from my paternal side of the family. Life was lonely at times, and all my little heart could focus on was having someone there to alleviate that loneliness. I prayed for a sibling like my life depended on it because, in my mind, it did. There were no neighborhood children to play with. The kids at church were just that—kids at church. I had not developed any significant peer relationships that were sustainable until college. I made do with books and writing and dreaming, but that only went so far. I often think of the questions I get about socialization when I mention to people that I homeschool my children. Going to a brick-and-mortar school, church, or any other activities does not guarantee socialization, and socialization definitely doesn't guarantee friendship.

Friendship is intentional.

As I began to find my way and cultivate friendships at the collegiate level, I wondered if I would ever have a close, white girlfriend again. Would having another close, white girlfriend ease the losses I had experienced, or was it just the overall longing for a close girlfriend regardless of her hue? There were so many things to consider. I went to denominational church schools for most of my educational upbringing, but that didn't protect me from thinly veiled racism from both teachers and students. We believe in the same Jesus and read the same Bible and worshipped on the same day—all things I thought would provide community, safety, and fellowship, fertile soil in which seeds of friendship can grow. But that wasn't quite my story.

Despite the challenges I faced, my optimism and pervasive love of people became a bridge between where I was and where I am now. It hasn't been an easy road, and I don't think I ever expected it to be such. But I knew that having any abiding, mutually beneficial friendship, in general, would mean a sacrifice of the old things. I would have to bury some of the pain I experienced in order to make room for opportunities that could change my heart and my position. I would have to surrender carrying that hurt with me, always peeking around life's corners and hovering just beneath the surface. At the time, I didn't realize that both grief and joy could coexist. I could sit in the reality of the sting of navigating loneliness, wanting friendship, but always having it slip through my fingers in one way or another. I could also revel in the fact that I was coming into my own, and that friendship wasn't some elusive, unattainable prize just out of reach. The belonging was what I brought with me, not something dependent on the presence or absence of someone else.

The tide began to turn. I leaned into this acknowledgment that belonging was something I brought with me, and I began to see myself as a friend worth having rather than someone who lacked friendships. I enjoy people. I love connection and community. I am a people gatherer, and I love to share the people I care for with others. Looking back, it's always been that way. Maybe because, in some ways, I was trying to create what I didn't have. Maybe if I could build that space, I too could benefit from it. Yet, there was also this nagging fear that not having friends (especially a best friend) meant something was broken in me. So, I invested in friendships, lots of them.

~

Years passed. I rejoiced every time I connected or reconnected with someone. I found healing and solace in so many areas. Grown-up friendships represented a new opportunity to form something deep, something lasting. My formerly starved heart would pitter-patter, and I hoped these relationships would be everything I ever wished for. It took time and patience and observance and a few more lessons learned that brought me nearer still to what real relationship was. It was in these early adult years that I built a foundation that became the springboard to many of my dearest friendships to date. It was like I had finally been given the cheat code to access unlimited simoleons (for all my Sims fans) in my own life. I was thriving.

However, in early 2020, life took several unexpected turns for my family. We took a huge leap of faith and relocated from Maryland to Atlanta, Georgia. We left a huge community and support system and a home where we regularly hosted family, friends, and neighbors, but I began to notice that the majority of that in-person community was Black. By this time, I also had a significant community of white friends as well, but almost all of them were online. I could count on less than one hand the relationships I had with white friends in-person. I had unintentionally grown an online presence full of wonderful, loving, white women, many of whom have leveraged their own platforms and networks to make room for me. They invited me to their virtual tables and into their hearts. This new space online allowed me to reconsider what it meant to be *friends* with white women, not just "friends." Many of those online relationships blossomed into a truth-telling, honest, and living friendship. Friendships rooted in a mutual love and respect for our differences in culture, upbringing, and our alignment in the dreams for our respective families. And just when one of those online relationships flipped into an in-person relationship, we left Maryland.

The year 2020 was a pivotal time not just in my life but in my community. Racial and political unrest littered the screens of television and social media, and suddenly everyone became a pundit, whether they had the expertise or not. We were a captive audience to people's opinions, and even more enlightening, we became privy to the dormant truths in the hearts of people we thought we knew well. Itchy ears turned toward what sounded good to them despite sound evidence and lived experience. Some of the relationships I thought were solidly formed on one set of commonalities dissipated like the steam coming up from a boiling pot of water. Was I losing white friendships again? Would it always be this way? No place felt safe. Lines were drawn across social media posts about voting preferences and bodily autonomy. I watched with horror as the internet emboldened vitriol in what I thought were the unlikeliest of places. For my mental well-being, I had to assess and reassign to acquaintance-ships relationships I thought were friendships.

Do I require all my friends and companions to think exactly the way I do? No. I do, however, expect that, as friends, we can agree to disagree without harm and the promotion of oppressive systems and institutions. Some of the people I was in relationship with at the time weren't able to do that, and that's okay too. One of the freedoms I learned in that season was that we get to choose how and where and when we enter into relationships with others. By the time I reached college, I had been so eager for so very long to have friendships that I would tiptoe around bad behavior like a parent trying to escape a sleeping toddler's room. In undergrad, these behaviors looked like highlighting my flaws in public when someone paid me a compliment, like commenting on the shape of my body in mixed company. And, in this new online space, it looked like wrapping rebukes up with out-of-context scripture references and testimonies. In both of these spaces, I wanted so badly for community to be maintained that I would accept performative, conditional relationships over actual, genuine care. It took a long time and a few "fallings-out" to unlearn those behaviors because I wanted so greatly to hold tightly to what I had been missing for so long. But that didn't work either. I used to feel really awkward when people would exclaim, "You know so many people!" I still do, at times, because I can't always tell if it's a compliment or something I should be ashamed of. What I know is that while I am grateful for one hundred pennies, I am much more comfortable at this point in my life with four quarters.

Today, I think I sit somewhere in between. Not bullied, not hoarding friends like acorns stuffed in squirrel cheeks. I enjoy this place. I have not given up on relationships with white women; I have a few abiding relationships that bring me joy. I have not given up on fulfilling relationships with Black women; I have some very solid relationships that have healed so much of the trauma I have experienced in the past. I treasure these life-changing friendships. The journey in all of this is a decidedly intentional choice to be a friend to myself first. Treating myself as good as I would any dear friend. Taking the time to enjoy my own company. Remembering to belong to myself. Owning my skin and the reflection I see in the mirror. I don't know where things will go from here, but I feel the excitement of belonging to me. This is the promise that came out of my perils.

14

Kathryn's Response

In Search of My Tribe

Kathryn V. Stanley

> *Where am I from? I'm from here . . . Originally? Well, I was born in Detroit, but I moved to DC when I was less than a year old, so I consider myself a native. My eyes? Well, these are my grandmother's eyes. She had hazel eyes too. I don't talk like a DC girl? Well, neither of my parents are from here. I don't talk "DC," but I do understand it VURRY well.*

The above is my side of conversations that I had during my formative years. Though maybe rooted in curiosity, the questions appeared to challenge my legitimacy among my own people, times when I was reminded that I didn't quite fit in.

I grew up in Washington, DC, when it was a predominantly Black city which sat in the shadow of a whole bunch of white monuments. Back then, it was known as "Chocolate City," and, though neither of my parents were from there and I wasn't born there, since I had my first birthday there, I call myself a native. We lived in a modest house in the upper Northwest quadrant in a largely working-class neighborhood. That meant nothing to me at the time. I just knew that there were lots of children in our community, and we all loved playing outside, riding bikes, jumping Double Dutch, and making mud pies. My first best friend was a girl with whom I went to nursery school and who also went to my first elementary school. She was as bony as I was thick. Her hair was long and wavy, while mine was short with a combination of textures. While she lived nearby, her family lived in an apartment building on a busy avenue which seemed worlds apart from where my family's house was. We played at each other's houses, though she came over to my house more often than I went to hers. Her parents were much older than mine, and she had grown brothers. I can still smell the combination of the dinner cooking in the hallway of her apartment building. Our parents weren't friends. They seemed to have little in common except having daughters the same age.

My parents' friend group was some families who attended the church where my dad was pastor. We spent most every holiday with them, and, though I have some fond memories of times with their children, I remember being teased, being the brunt of cruel jokes. Yet, something within me continued longing for their acceptance. While there were times when I secretly dreaded going, I had no other choice. These were the people with whom my parents had found their belonging. Surprisingly, I often longed to live closer to them—perhaps so I would feel more accepted.

When my dad decided the family needed to move to what was known as the "Black Gold Coast" in closer proximity to many of the families he pastored, we moved to the same neighborhood as my parents' friends, and I changed schools. The community of friends I had made in our old neighborhood was largely left behind. I don't recall asking, but I don't remember my parents making an effort to help maintain those connections through birthday party invitations or playdates. If they did, it didn't last long.

The move was not what I expected. The school I had longed to attend in the neighborhood where my parents' friends sent their children was a culture shock. While the racial demographic was similar to the old neighborhood, the socioeconomics seemed worlds apart. These were children of DC's Black elite, Du Bois's Talented Tenth, some "new money," some old, many of whom were benefiting from being the "Black firsts" in fields that just recently had been pried open in the post-1960s civil rights world.

I was one of two new students in a class of sixty children. We were what was called then an "open" classroom taught by a team of two teachers. That alone felt intimating. When I stood up to introduce myself wearing my new dress from the "chubby" section of Sears, I remember hearing snickers because apparently my dress rode up on my booty.

The children of the elite were well aware of their privilege. The popular girls bragged about shopping at Lord & Taylor, Bloomingdale's, and Neiman Marcus. Where I had come from, Sears was our "go to" and perhaps Woodie's or Hecht's for special occasions. In my old neighborhood, kids teased other kids about shopping at Morton's, a discount clothing chain located in DC's Black neighborhoods. I would soon find that in the new neighborhood shopping at Sears was a source of ridicule.

I remember the most popular girl in school approaching me, a girl who bragged about the number of valentines she received while giving none. My longing for acceptance caused me to jump at the opportunity to be seen in conversation with her. She asked me, "Where do you get your clothes?" Though her conversational tone didn't read as teasing, it was clear that my answer to this question would solidify myself as one of "them" or not. I don't recall my initial response; maybe I named stores like Woodie's or Hecht's because, while not high end, they were middle range and somewhat respectable. My response to her second question, "Do your parents ever buy your clothes from Sears?" I recall very clearly. "Sometimes," I said half-smiling and realizing that she had the ammunition she needed to place me outside of the "in" crowd. My being one of the smart kids in the class didn't matter because I was the fat kid whose parents bought her clothes from Sears.

There was one group of girls with whom I found some belonging: the girls' kickball team. I had played kickball since I could remember. The rules were simple. It didn't require a high level of hand-eye coordination, and my awkward left-handedness didn't matter. Though I wasn't particularly athletic, I joined the team anyway—especially since I had a secret crush on Mr. Johnson, the PE teacher and coach. These girls didn't care where anyone shopped; they were all about playing the game. We'd hop on the bus to go to our games, and I felt like I was back in my old neighborhood again.

The junior high years were a mixed bag. It marked the first time I went to a school that had more than a handful of white people. And because my mother signed me up for the advanced classes, it was the first time I was one of the only Black children in my class. I still stood out because I was smart, something I loved to rock because it seemed to make up for what I and others considered my less-than-ideal body size.

At recess, I would connect with my Black friends. We'd jump Double Dutch and share the latest gossip. I felt as though I could use my "Black voice" with them—though some of them still told me I spoke "white." This was my introduction to "code switching." I often heard my mom use her "white" voice on the telephone with customer service or other places where she was seeking support. I suppose a vestige of her having grown up in segregated America is that being white, and therefore, sounding white, had its privileges.

Belonging, fitting in, feeling seen is a basic human need. Having a sense of community, a place to call "home" is something that most of us long for. For Black Americans, belonging has been a complicated notion. Our forced removal from Africa to what would become the United States of America ripped us of our collective sense of ancestral belonging. And yet, the country which we built limited our belonging to cotton, tobacco, and rice fields. Still, we somehow found ways to build community among each other, to create hush harbors where worship occurred, where we knew we belonged to God when seemingly everyone or everything else had been stripped from us. Upon emancipation, many of us went in search of family members who had been sold away, while others decided to "stay put." There's a certain comfort with staying in a place you know. Since then we have demanded "belonging," screaming, "I, too, am America" along with Langston Hughes.[1]

To be sure, my Black is less common. I didn't realize that being the child, grandchild, great-grandchild, and great-great-grandchild of college graduates was a rarity among most people, but especially among Black people. My parents didn't raise me to believe that my "elite pedigree" made me better than others. Instead, it meant that we had a generational responsibility to uplift the race. And our access didn't mean that we were shielded from white terror. In some ways, we were more exposed to it. Despite my upbringing, there have still been times when I had to check my own privilege vis-a-vis Black people whose social location did not afford them the same experiences I had.

In retrospect, I conflated acceptance with belonging. Acceptance often requires a person to suppress her authentic self which may result in a sense of belonging in a temporal sense. But as soon as the standard for belonging shifts, as soon as acceptance requires something else, something new, something different, self shifts again.

The assumption that belonging is automatic based on race was something I learned early on not to be true. There are ways in which many Black people have shared experiences around race and racism, and there is indeed evidence of Black culture cues—both formed on this side of the ocean and retained from our original home—that if you know, you know. But there are still ways in which we, too, have created a "kitchen" similar to the one Hughes refers to in "I, Too!" that white people put us in. Maybe the desire to belong is so strong that once we find it, we feel the only way to keep it is to deny others their sense of belonging.

At various points in my life, I have been met with questions which may have been born out of curiosity but, for me, felt as though my belonging was being challenged or questioned by what I thought was my own tribe—Black people. I never expected to "fit in" with white people, though there was a time I thought it was important to try. When I entered education and work spaces where there were white people, I often felt the need to defy stereotypes of Black women. I didn't want to be considered "too aggressive," "too loud," or too anything else that played into their narrative. There is a sense in which being my authentic self was stifled by the white gaze. But it was the longing for belonging from my own that I wanted more than anything.

Yet, at some point, as I grew and matured, the need to fit in subsided. I can't quite say when this happened, but I even came to understand that not fitting in is a virtue—especially when it means advocating for the belonging of those who have been systematically excluded. Over time, I realized that what I was really looking for more than anything was the ability to authentically live into the many facets of my identity. I didn't find this in a group. Instead, I found it in myself. I became less concerned about "finding my tribe" and more committed to living into the woman God made me.

I often wonder what became of that girl who teased me for shopping at Sears. I haven't seen her since we left elementary school. She, like so many others from those days, went on to elite private secondary schools. I wonder if she ever experienced moments in those spaces where her family's money was a drop in the bucket compared to others. I wonder if she ever learned that shopping sprees can't outshop the assumptions that others make about Black women.

I know what became of that girl who got teased for shopping at Sears. She grew to despise anything that sniffs of elitism, to wear hand-me-downs from other people's closets or thrift stores, to embrace her own Blackness as an authentic form, and to have a playlist that's both righteous and ratchet. She became one who "found God in herself and loved her fiercely."[2]

Notes

1. Langston Hughes, "I, Too," Poetry Foundation, accessed October 14, 2023, https://www.poetryfoundation.org/poems/47558/i-too.

2. Ntozake Shange, *For Colored Girls Who Have Considered Suicide, When the Rainbow Is Enuf: A Choreopoem* (New York: MacMillan, 1977).

15

Seven Stones

Patrice Gopo

I awake in the dusky hours when shadowed memories swallow the room. A hushed silence stirs around me, a distant car engine breaking the stillness as I turn and turn again. Puncturing the night, a white friend's remembered voice, her recent declaration to me about the root of our disagreement. "Patrice, you're not seeing things clearly." Her tone even and straightforward, but the words sharp against my ears. "But I am," she went on to say as if I were a child throwing a tantrum, and she the adult.

These interruptions have become my companion, a return to sleep eluding me the longer I ponder my friend's . . . What? What would the word be? *Boldness? Audacity? Hubris?* Tonight, in the groggy quiet, as with past nights and nights still to come, I place this friendship and others with white women beneath the burden of middle-of-the-night ruminating. The ones where conflict ripped into the health of the relationship and left it fractured. This waking pattern is the place where I poke and prod at the friendships. The mind mulls, and the body cannot rest. In these states of ruptured sleep, I pile on the questions, the what-ifs, the mysteries of the past. *Why did these friendships break?*

To wake, though, is to also recall goodness I can name: the way we could converse about a topic for hours, how we could engage with the reality of racial brokenness and injustice, how we watched each other's children, how we supported each other's work endeavors, how we gave each other gifts steeped in thoughtfulness and meaning, how we laughed and laughed, how we took long walks, how we helped empower each other to speak up and take hard—but necessary—action, how we prayed together and ate together and welcomed the intersection of our lives. It is as if everything about these friendships were piled on a scale, the goodness weighing the scale toward health. And yet none of this could overcome the reality of so much else. *None of this goodness could be enough to counter the impact of what?* I ask myself that night and other nights, the question slipping into my daytime thinking, the question finding me during my morning walks, as I watch a television show, when I'm sweeping the kitchen floor. *The impact of conflict.* My whispered words become a shout within.

And in the night, I see stones. Stones placed as counterweights to all that was good. Stones that intensify the impact of any conflict. Stones that tilt the plate further from health, past equilibrium, cracking fissures, dragging the creaking scale into the firm realm of fragmentation. There are stones, each with a weight of its own.

Stone One: Discomfort

Moments after I arrived at the community event, a friend told me that a Black woman had just called her "an entitled white woman." Around where we stood on the lawn, children laughed, families wandered to the various stations, and people lined up for hot dogs—the air was draped in the yawning casualness of outdoor celebration. My friend shared the story, the contours of her eyes wider than normal, her face taking on shock. And I felt the thing I have felt before, the queasy squishing discomfort that overtakes me as I witness a friend's confusion, maybe even pain. My rush to eliminate the tension of this moment.

After asking a few questions, I told her what I would want to hear, what might move us past this awkward moment, perhaps what I hoped might be true: "I'm sure it had nothing to do with you and was more about what she's working through." My response sprung forth, unrestrained, without the time needed to determine if my words were accurate or a statement I believed. There would come days in the future when I would cluster this moment with so many other moments. As I sat at the edge of the couch in my therapist's office, as I spilled endless blue ink in my journal, as I walked my daily path, I would consider all the ways I split myself apart, declaring out loud what I might realize later didn't align with my thinking. All in the name of eliminating the pain in another. And the discomfort in me.

In the future, I would probe this ancient pattern of mine. I would fall back to early memories and see the ways I avoided hard moments with others and with me. I would observe how reshaping an interaction to reflect positivity could draw people toward me. A Black girl in a childhood saturated with white. To use words to cushion another's discomfort eliminated tension and brought people near me. There in the grass, I was still many years from discovering how my discomfort was not an enemy. Instead, discomfort was a friend warning me of my propensity to wrap my sense of safety in my white friend's well-being. Awareness of my discomfort would become the very thing to begin liberating me.

"I'm sure it had nothing to do with you," I quickly told my friend that day. My attempt to soothe a stranger's blistering words and preserve a temporary harmony.

Stone Two: Labor

A friend and I stood by my kitchen counter, draining the final sips of tea in mugs now gone cool to the touch. Shortly, we would hug each other and say good-bye until a future visit. In those closing moments, we crammed in final thoughts, the last story, the last idea. This friend expressed feelings of hesitancy about how others might interpret her marriage to a Black man. She wondered if people realize she is engaged with justice issues and not just a white woman who snatched up a Black man. My friend came to me to reassure her. As I listened, I formed an answer in my head, a recipe I built that wouldn't create distance in this friendship: one part comfort and reassurance, another part patience and calm, a third part with just a sprinkling of truth or conviction—a bit vague, though, to protect me in case my words caused offense. My mind made a quick connection to another story I'd read about a couple whose appearance led people to assume something about them that wasn't true. I shared the story and finished with, "People might think, but you don't have control." She nodded her head, her face that once expressed worry softening into peace.

And after she walked out of my home, I was left with her question and my reply. I was left with my wonder if my words were kind or harsh and with my weariness at formulating such responses. Given her questions, given the energy it took to answer, could such a friendship bask in the warmth of mutuality? I look back, and I struggle to see such a possibility. But words are a strange thing, the way the heft of lopsided labor was then not a part of my vocabulary.

Back then, I offered the words she viewed as wise and reassuring just as I'd offered them in the past and likely as I'd offer them in the future. Back then, I assumed such work was just the cost of maintaining this friendship.

Stone Three: Shame

On an early summer day when the trees had embraced—in total—the thick green of the season, a friend told me, "If I don't throw myself on the floor, filled with remorse, you won't accept my apology." Deep in the middle of unresolved conflict, our interactions had descended into exhausted attempts at making the other person understand our perspective and experience. During one of those circular conversations that produced little change or results, I walked in the late morning, the heat of summer already burning into my skin. My friend joined me through the phone line. *Throw myself on the floor. Filled with remorse. Won't accept apology.* Her words rooted me in place, unable to take the next step, the patches of clouds shifting slightly above me. "When have I ever asked that of you?" My question created a pause after which she replied, "No, you haven't asked that of me."

I heard a story once about someone who mediates conflicts at a university. The particular job and location matter little to this story. What stood out, though, and has remained with me is this person's ability to mediate conflict across races and genders, to mediate conflict between almost anyone. "Except Black women and white women," the teller of the story explained. "Apparently, white women feel like they are already doing so much, they struggle to believe it isn't enough." And I wondered if masked beneath the surface of a white woman envisioning that she was doing so much was the shame that perhaps she wasn't doing enough?

Later, in the hours, days, weeks, and months that followed that conversation with my friend, much later when the tension in my body relaxed into clearer thinking and the summer green had disappeared for another year, I wondered how responsible I could be for someone else's feelings that arose beyond reality. I was powerless against the scenario she chose to believe. Outside my control was the way her sense of shame crept in and landed on me.

Stone Four: Offerings

In the final episode of the *Queen's Gambit*, Jolene and Beth, the white friend, sit against the wall of a gymnasium, the aftermath of a racquetball game. Jolene, Beth's long-ago friend from their shared orphanage days. Jolene, who has not appeared in the previous five episodes and the last decade of Beth's life. And poof! Just like that, Jolene falls back on tropes about being family and solves Beth's problem. She offers Beth the money she's been saving for law school. At first a protest from Beth and then she accepts this rescue move.

"Jolene, how stupid are you?" I said to the screen. "Jolene, how stupid are you?" And there with the iPad propped up on a pillow in front of me, there as this Black friend rushed in with what she had of value to support her white friend's dream, the tears arrived. A smattering at first and then more and more, ribbons of saltwater on my face. "You didn't have to accept," I said to Beth who, of course, could not engage with this one-sided conversation. "You didn't have to accept." Beth, who owns a house. Beth, who could use it, leverage it, and refuse her friend's savings.

The tears that fell were about Jolene and not Jolene. The tears that fell were about Beth and not Beth too. What had I offered at the altar of friendship that I never should have offered? What offering had my white friends accepted that they should never have taken? Why take my offering from me when they could have taken from the bounty of what they already had? And later I would hear a podcast episode state, "People of color are often times more oriented to make sure white people are taken care of before they take care of themselves."[1] I would hear those words and nod knowingly. I would think of my own stories and wonder if this act is a reflex to ensure relational safety.

As the saltwater cascaded, I said to myself once more, "How stupid are you, Jolene?" In truth, this was a question turned inward, a question intended for me.

Stone Five: Optimism

"I'm so scared I will say something that will hurt you," a friend told me. In the days following the Charleston Church Massacre, this white friend and I shared a meal. The fast-food restaurant bustled with the movement of people finding seats, trays being cleared from the table, the quick pace of consumption. My friend and I sat and talked as if this were a coffee shop made for slow conversation. Worry and concern gripped her voice. "So scared," she repeated.

"If that happens, I think we'd figure a way through," I replied. We'd first begun such conversations six months prior, on a wide lawn, in the aftermath of a grand jury refusing to indict the police officer who killed

Michael Brown. We stood just beyond the shade cast by a soaring tree. A mild day in December as people gathered for a community lunch. She'd invited me to let our blossoming friendship expand that day, to shift from the place of conversations about work and family to now letting the topic of race be something we might together consider. My friend, who perhaps then was just beginning to seem like a person I wanted for a friend, had asked me if we could talk about what was happening. That day, we stood in the grass, slivers of chill pricking the sunshine pleasant on my skin. On that day, I voiced some version of, "Sure, okay," speaking words that might encourage the growth of this friendship. This friendship expansion began with her request and proceeded with my positive response.

"If that happens, I think we'd figure a way through," I replied half a year later in the fast-food restaurant—my attempt to put my friend at ease about her worry and my trust in the foundation we'd built. I said those words to her two days after the brutal murder of nine Black people. I said all this having no idea what the future would bring, how much hurt could happen, how naïve my words might be. I could not envision this friend's struggle to recognize all that society might place at her feet because of her skin. And most of all, I could not yet articulate my belief that my friend's fear was not a fear of hurting me. Instead, it was a fear of feeling shame because she said or did something damaging. I believe this now because doesn't true fear about hurting me seek to repair when I point out how that is happening?

"We would figure a way through," I repeated, emphasizing what—for too long—I would believe.

Stone Six: Her Expectations (of Me)

. . . that I would comfort her in her distress that I would be loyal with less consideration for my own welfare that I would offer wise thoughts and healing words that I would offer wise thoughts and healing words that I would offer wise thoughts and healing words that I would speak in a tone she considered soft and gentle that I would talk about race when she wanted to but not when she didn't want to that I would remain calm and even if addressing injustice within our friendship that I would not address injustice within our friendship without her permission that I would be content with her determining what is a valid complaint and what is me just seeing the situation incorrectly that I would have no issues with her rewriting the past to frame her as the hero that I would listen to her stories—perhaps at the expense of telling mine that I would be there for her that I wouldn't say or do anything that might trigger her feelings of shame that I would speak in a way that she perceived as full of grace that I would that I would that I would that I would that I would . . .

But why not walk away?

. . . because of the memory of what had been because I am a Black woman and not just a Black woman because she could connect with a particular angle of me because of the times she saw me because of the parts of our stories that spoke to a similar history because something in her called to life something that had been dormant in me because maybe I long for all aspects of me to live and that needs the presence of many because that part that once came alive has returned to dormancy because to lose a friend is to lose a particular way I existed in the world because mixed within the hard were layers of beauty because the pain I felt was that of a heart breaking because of the memory of what had been because of the memory of what had been because of the memory of what had been . . .

Stone Seven: Absence

One Easter morning, many years after the fracturing of these friendships I thought had a firm foundation, I had a dream. A dream on a day flooded with the image of a boulder rolled from the entrance of an empty tomb. A dream that began in some sort of Bible theology class—or was it a church?—and moved to a white friend standing just beyond the sanctuary. A white friend with whom I had never found a way back to how our friendship once was. In the Easter morning dream, she told me that she had been waiting for me and wanted to apologize. "I'm sorry for treating you in such a condescending way," this dream friend said to me, her words a bright turquoise against the muted colors of the dreamscape. There was the humble cadence of her voice. There was her statement spoken as if the initial notes in the first movement of all that still needed to unfold with this apology. And there was the dream version of me who started to cry. After all these years, I knew we could not return to the friendship we once had. Perhaps, though, there existed a chance for increased peace. We both hugged and made our way through a brightly lit atrium edged with great pots holding birds of paradise, the enormous green leaves a striking tableau in the sunlit room. We walked toward a place—where I can't say but only felt—holding the promise of a restituted future. And the people. The other people. We passed people we both knew, familiar faces from moments in our shared past, children and adults as well, all grouped around a glass table. People who waved as if they too had been waiting for a very long time.

When I awoke, though, I knew the images, the apology, the side-by-side journey, all this had been just a dream. The mind is always active and searches for remedies. But these words had not transpired. These were not actual steps toward what could be. Instead, just the ability of my unconscious mind to name my lingering longing. Longing for what? Maybe acknowledgment of wounding. Or the mere simplicity of resolution. Perhaps I still wanted to imagine that there existed such a boulder that could crush the weight of each stone, grinding it to dust, letting the particles disappear in the breeze.

Note

1. David Bailey. "Communal Suffering: Can These Bones Live?" *Strengthening the Soul of Your Leadership*. Podcast audio, March 27, 2023. https://ruthhaleybarton.podbean.com/e/season-19-lent-week-5-communal-suffering-can-these-bones-live/.

16

Chichi's Response

Decentering Discomfort in Two Letters

CHICHI AGOROM

To Discomfort, In Defense of My Sisters

You have a sneaky way of sucking up all the air in the room, Discomfort. When you appear with your big frame and your gaping mouth and your fingers poised to squeeze and squeeze and squeeze till you reign supreme, you make it seem like nothing else is possible, like nothing else is true. You've almost always gotten what you want, Discomfort. You want to be the first, to be the loudest, to be the only thing that matters.

You are not the only thing that matters. Matter of fact, you do not reign supreme. You aren't unimportant, but you do need to learn your place.

How it is that you manage to convince people to bend to your will is astonishing. You have us all convinced that we must appease you, make you feel comfortable, feed our true desires and longings into your gaping mouth so that *we* can survive. What are we left with, then, when we have fed our wholeness to you for survival? What can we be proud of when it is your agenda we have prioritized, not our own?

You convince us that the only way to breathe again is by appeasing you. Each time we feed our truth into your gaping mouth, you release a breath of air back into the room. Grateful, we gasp the relief into our lungs, and with it, the lie that surrendering our truth was the right thing to do. Each breath you return to us is laced with poison, poison that settles like lead in our lungs. We're still breathing, yes, but we are doomed. We are still breathing, yes, but we host a graveyard in our lungs of the things we needed to say, the truth that hung suspended in the air that you took. We are still breathing, yes, but shallow, unable to reach the depths clogged by your poison.

You seem to disappear once you are appeased, but you are never truly gone. Lurking, translucent, waiting for the right moment to appear again and demand our truth, our wholeness as an offering. A never satiated dictator-god who cares only for more at the expense of all.

I'm writing to you to say: I see through you. Translucent as you try to be in the quiet moments, I am not fooled by you. You do not scare me, with your gaping mouth the size of eternity, ready to swallow our full being if we let you. And that's the thing, isn't it? We don't have to let you.

Of course, it doesn't *feel* like we have a choice when you take up all the air and we are choking on our desperate desire to survive. But that is part of the lie you feed us, that we do not get to choose. Only to appease. What happens if we don't appease you? Do you wither and die? Do you loom even larger, inflated by your indignation?

I know that you do not die, Discomfort. For as much as I'd like to send seven stones flying at your face, you should not die. When you take the form of a teacher and not a monster, you can lead us into wider pastures where we see more clearly and know more fully. You show us the lies we are believing and the ways in which we can grow. So, you should not die because we would not grow.

But when you collaborate with the powerfully wielded fragility of white women, when you inhabit their bodies and minds so wholly, *that* is what turns you into a monster capable of destruction. Like a mind-controlling parasite bending an organism's body to its will, you demand satiation through their tears, through their shock that they are not being perceived as the good, innocent girls they think they are.

You lie to them, Discomfort, convincing them that they cannot survive you, that they must give what you demand. They believe you, and, in turn, cause us harm just to appease and satiate you. Not just that, they use their power to coerce us Black women into satisfying you, making the alleviation of the discomfort *they* are feeling *our* responsibility.

A society that caters to the comfort of white women, ensuring that they are always protected, teaches us that when discomfort arises in the body of a white woman nothing else matters more than appeasing that discomfort. So, we contort ourselves into painful and unnatural shapes to appease so that we do not die. It doesn't matter that we are now left disfigured by the contorting we do to keep them from harming us. It doesn't matter that we never get to experience comfort in their presence. What matters is that we do what we *must* to survive, as we have always done.

What must die, then, isn't you but this belief white women hold that they cannot survive you. That we must protect them from you by becoming smaller, less threatening, more amiable. I know that you are survivable, and it is that knowing that silences my fear. But you work overtime to keep them from realizing that they, too, can survive you.

Learn your place, Discomfort. We will not be coerced by you or those under your spell anymore. Our liberation is too delicious and inviting, and we choose to no longer starve ourselves just to keep you satisfied.

To Patrice, In Solidarity

I see you. The exhaustion you must feel carrying those stones with you. The pain you feel at recognizing the imbalance in your relationships. The labor of having to rearrange your truth to ease their discomfort. The burden of always needing to be wise and calm even when anger is the most appropriate response. The grief that arises at the realization that while you have held space for all of their becomings, they cannot hold space for yours. The longing for them to take accountability; for your experiences and your pain to matter just as much as their avoidance of shame. The broken-heartedness over all the things you have lost, the things you offered to people who were not deserving of them.

I see you. I am with you. You are not alone.

We always do what we need to do to keep ourselves safe, to maintain a sense of okay-ness, even if it means swallowing our truth. Maybe because we do it so frequently and with the appearance of effortlessness, it looks to outsiders like it is of no consequence to us. Like it is easy. Like it has no impact on our wellbeing. Like it is one of our applaudable strengths. Like we even enjoy doing it.

As Zora Neale Hurston said, "If you are silent about your pain, they will kill you and say you enjoyed it." But sometimes they try to kill you for being loud about your pain, for naming the thing that they don't want to see or change. It takes courage—and an immense amount of energy—to let the truth out, to name your pain out loud, especially as a Black woman. So, I am proud to stand as a witness to your truth-telling, no matter what comes after. I rejoice with you in the freedom that is found through telling the truth of your full humanity. All the versions of Patrice, who were not offered the safety to be fully true, rejoice as well.

Of course, the internal and external voices that tell you to minimize your pain will continue to arise. But please remember that your pain is valid, appropriately-sized, not too much, not made up. Even if they never acknowledge it as real, you can always practice telling the truth to yourself. We know that they would rather dismiss our pain than be honest about the harm they cause, which is both infuriating and painful. And yet, what I hope for all of us—difficult as it may be—is that we begin prioritizing our freedom over their understanding or validation. I want us to prioritize our wellness and rest over easing their discomfort.

It has never been your job to hold their discomfort as well as your own. Their feelings are not your emergency. Each of us has an individual responsibility to learn how to be with discomfort rather than run from it, how to look it in the face and ask questions of it, letting it guide us to something true. You are responsible for your own relationship with discomfort. But protecting them from their own discomfort? That has never been your responsibility. We do not have to continue to be the world's mule.

Instead, take a deep breath. Feel your feet on the ground. Let your attention slowly caress the length of your spine. Feel the sturdiness of your back and think of all who have your back—past, present, physical, spiritual—and let them remind you that you are enough and you are not alone. And then, fortified by that practice, let those white women choke on their own discomfort. It is the only way they will learn how to survive it.

We survive discomfort and pain every day. They applaud us and call us *resilient*. I don't believe that resilience is our highest good; it is simply just stating that we are capable of surviving the worst without dying and with intuitive intelligence. I want a world for us where we are at rest, at ease, playful, lighthearted, protected, and free. One way we can make that freedom a practice rather than a dreamed-of utopia is to refuse to keep protecting white women from their own discomfort and shame. Let them do their work, so we can focus on our work of freedom and ease and joy.

For your consideration:

Stone Eight: Love

Not a stone but a boulder that causes the earth to shake as it moves, its massive size formed by the enduring love and solidarity of your sisters who see you and get you and believe you and support you.

> *The solid weight of Black women's love moves towards you with enough power to crush those stones of absence, expectations, optimism, offerings, shame, labor, and discomfort into dust.*

No matter how many new stones are formed or how many old stones recover their shape, you are a part of something larger and more powerful, the force of which can change the world. The next time you awake in the night, remember that you always have the boulder on your side.

17

A Closed Forum

Q & A

Kadeisha M. Bonsu

Opening Address: I have been so afraid to release the minutes from this forum into the world for public access; however, what I now see as the Recorder is that these minutes are vitally necessary. In just the first page of this transcript, I see that I once was too tired to honor my capacity by giving myself required permission to release my own internalized defense of white fragility in the name of self-preservation. I felt guilty in the wake of this record of Forum minutes because I feared the words would hurt my white friends of the heart. Those white folks who have been genuinely good to me but, like all of us, suffer the sins of our fleshly existence and our dusty humanity. But ultimately, what remains true is that it's not my job to take responsibility for their wrongdoings, and that these forum notes, representing our authentic collective conversation, vitally invite our white counterparts to make their amends. If you can move past the initial hurt, pain, or offense you may feel, you may find in these words a gift. A love offering of "what not to do" so that you might more accurately discern "what *to* do." I pray that you hear these words as if that of a prophecy. I pray that as you read these words you may experience them as A Word of the Lord for Woke [but oblivious] White Women. A Word of the Lord for White feminists who believe themselves to be down with the people. A Word of the Lord for Miss Sally, Karen, and 'nem. A word of the Lord for you.

Therefore, Hear the Word of the Lord . . .

Moderator 1: Please state the purpose of this forum for the record, its nature, and participants present.

Moderator 2: This forum was convened to address DIY reparations initiated in 2020 by white liberals, presumably trying to right the wrongs of their ancestors. They were well intentioned perhaps, but clearly uninformed about how to organize. To that end, my Black Sisters and I are asking ourselves questions and struggling through answers about how our white Sisters gathered in caucuses across the globe to heal their white guilt and wipe their fragile white tears, tears that we Black women refused to keep handing out tissues for. To begin, I'll offer some words of context for our white Sisters for the purposes of when these forum notes are released:

> Dear Sisters,
> If you're wondering why we have yet to connect with you, quite honestly, We is ti'ed. We were unwilling to let you continue to exhaust us. So tired in fact that we don't even have the energy to code switch.
>
> Your fragility, treated like a *porcelain doll*, wearied our hearts and minds.
>
> I remember the moment we all started getting those notifications:
>
> $20: Self-care
>
> $10: Do something nice for yourself.
>
> $15: I can't imagine what you all are going through.
>
> $10: I'm so sorry!
>
> THAT'S a sorry apology! Pathetic!
>
> But, we protected your fragility because we ourselves were too heartbroken and weary to engage.
>
> So, we write to our Sisters, collectively and individually. I will talk to my Sister, though you are many. We write to the one on behalf of the whole.
>
> Sister, I like us. I like our friendship. I've felt the love between us grow over these years.
>
> Sister, I love you. I love us. I love our friendship.
>
> But this! This really hit.
>
> You're allowed to make mistakes. To get it wrong.
>
> But any Sister of mine knows that we may brawl, but the apology better make up for it.
>
> Making amends is a part of the bond.
>
> You never extended so much as an apology.
>
> You broke the Sister code.

I am grieved that it has come to this.

I pray that we can make amends, and I hope that this won't be the end.

But if it is, I loved you, Sister—and I still do!

We have read this letter on behalf of one of our Sistahs, in solidarity but also because it aptly summarizes a shared concern among us all. To that end, this closed forum of Black Women is officially commenced so that we might all ask the questions we often entertain in our own heads but rarely have the space or energy to articulate. It is a mosaic of questions to ourselves, to our white female counterparts, and it is our general ponderings. Those present are Black women invitees, only so that we can have the necessary safety and space to express ourselves freely and without fear of retribution. Nevertheless, we want to acknowledge that though this is a closed forum, the meeting minutes will be made public and available for comment in hopes that our white allies will read them, heed them, and grow from them.

Moderator 1: We'll take our first question . . .

Q: Did they call a forum on "Reparations for your Black friends?"

A: I don't know what secret committee of white folks gathered and decided to use their petty cash for reimbursement to their "Black friends."

But 2020 was the year.

It happened in 2020.

What didn't happen in 2020?

2020, the year that [fill in the blank].

2020 . . .

The year my grandparents died,

The year of the plague that took them,

The year I rested from unreasonable standards of labor,

The year we missed our baby's first rite of passage because we couldn't host a first birthday party due to social distancing.

2020, the year of *Venmo*, *Cash App*, and *Zelle* alerts.

Ping.

Sara just sent you $20.

Q: What are these itty-bitty Venmos supposed to do? Is this supposed to absolve you from your guilt? I won't withdraw it . . . should I?

A: I let that money sit in Venmo for at least six months.

It sat. I sat with pain.
It sat. I sat with anger.
It sat. I sat with confusion.
It sat. I tried to understand.
It sat. I questioned myself.
It sat. The damages accrued.

Q: What was the transaction fee passed to the consumer?

A: A million little cuts too benign for anyone to see or treat.

So-called microaggressions.

What are microaggressions anyway?

My mama'nem use to keep it simple and just call a spade a spade: racism.

But this day, we know a "woke" person by their diction, i.e. "microaggression."

You are *really* a disruptor though, when you turn it into a verb: "microaggressed."

Q: What's a microaggression? Can I use it in a sentence?

A: Sure!

Karen microaggressed against the Black man who was enjoying bird watching and minding his own business.[1]

Q: Is it really micro?

A: Herein lies my problem with the word "microaggression."

It softens the blow and somehow softens the perceived sense of impact and accountability.

What did Karen really do?

Karen verbally assaulted an innocent, kind, compassionate Black man whom she assumed to be threatening because of his beautiful, kissed-by-the-sun, warm tones of brown melanated flesh.

So, is Karen a microaggressor or a racist?

Q: Whhhyyyy do white folks think these things are okay?

A: My guess is it soothes white guilt? Please have them let us know once they read the minutes. I don't have time to address white fragility and make sense of it. They can do their work, and I'll do mine.

Q: What's the difference between intent and impact?

A: Whatever this secret meeting of white folks was, while money for "self-care" in the wake of George Floyd's murder and on the first federally recognized Juneteenth might sound thoughtful, it is a slap in the face "with a knick-knack-paddy-whack-give-a-dog-a-bone" kinda vibe.

Perhaps, they really only see us as worthy of being thrown a bone. But I side with the Syrophoenician woman who appealed to Jesus on this one[2] . . . If I, as a Black woman, could be treated as good as their dogs, I might actually stand a chance of living.

I mean for real. . . . We probably have more white animal rights activists than the performative *Black Lives Matter* signs on your lawn.

Q: What could Sister have done differently?

A: "*It*" never came up.

She's one of my best friends, and I love her dearly, but 'til today, it never came up.

We have had numerous phone calls since then.

Don't you want to know if I got your money?

Do you wonder why I haven't said *thank you*?

Or, do you all somehow feel resolved just fulfilling your annual tax write-off for your noble deeds?

I just wanted you to say something . . . break the ice, so to speak . . . so that I didn't have to keep carrying your burdens with no offer for you to carry some of mine.

You know how many times I've just wanted white folks to say something?

We teach kids about bullying and the bystander effect as we've all likely heard, "If you see something, say something," and still, I know countless white folks who become hard-of-hearing and visually impaired when it matters most. It is only now that I realize that it's possible we have talked less and less because you do have a sense that your Venmo offerings were not so well received. Could it be that your guilt has imprisoned you to self-shame and condemnation leading to disconnecting rather than your intuition and discernment of the matter leading to repentance that invites deeper relationship? The potential of promise, the real hope of promise, but the pain of perils.

Q: So that our white allies can better understand, can one of us elaborate on the following: What was it like going through the aftermath of Venmo reparations? How has this impacted you?

A: I feel sick writing this.
Tightening in chest.
Clenching in jaw.
Knots in stomach.
Hyper . . .
Breathe . . .
Ventilate . . .
Breathe . . .
Searching for breath.
Feet on ground.
In, breathe in.
Out, shake it out.
Worry creeping up my spine.
Fear raising up the hair on my arms.
But we don't talk about our unspoken panic attacks.
We all collectively draw our breath in.
We slowly push our breath back out.

We draw a short breath back in, feeling the tiny black hairs stand up on the back of our dark skin.

We let that breath out in a quick, gut-suckering, chest-clinching release.

In real fast.
Out with barely enough air.
I, too, can't breathe.
While you let out a sigh of, "At least I sent that Venmo."
In, jaw tightening.
Out, stomach knotting.
In, hand to my chest, looking for breath.
Out, I grab my shirt in my sweaty palm, clenching.
In, breathe.
Feet on ground.
Out, shake it out.
I won't withdraw it.
In.
"Girl, you betta use that money!"
Out.

We never talked about it.

We are still friends.

But we don't talk about our unspoken panic attacks.

We don't . . . lest we be triggered.

Lest I drop your *porcelain doll.*

Lest I bring it up at the dinner table that we only just now started being invited to.

But this table?

At this table I sit.

Do you understand what it's like to be gasping for air?

To cry for your mama 'cause you can't breathe?

But maybe Mama is unavailable, cause she's nursing your white babies.

And on that note, I'm tired of taking care of white women crying like babies.

At this table I sit.

Pull up a chair if you dare.

Q: What helps you keep going?

A: I sit at the table for Carrie Lee Bass.

I sit at the table for Nathan Butler, and many more who were only ever good enough to set the table and serve, but never to dine at the table.

I sit down.

I sit down for those who could not.

But I don't keep quiet.

They would have been glad for just a seat.

But I? I speak up, I speak out.

It is the reason I speak these words in this forum though somewhat terrified and nervous for the day we release them to the world for public comment.

Q: I'm left sitting here wondering can a white girl ever truly be a Sistah?

A: I'll answer this by addressing my Sister directly. Sister, I write this piece for you and many other white friends that I never dared to think of as a Sistah. But yours is the ultimate betrayal, because I've always wanted to give you an honorary "Sis."

I didn't 'cause I feared that would be fraudulent.

That sentiment frustrated me because I really think you're a "real one."

But none of us, *none*, are exempt from our history.

We don't have to be our past, but you can't be a better present you without healing your past and properly integrating it and making amends for past transgressions.

Sister, I've had to force myself to remember. I've had to remind myself not to fall prey to the bait of the white illusion of color-blindness. Having done such, I've compelled myself to remember that you are still white. You are my friend who is white. And, hopefully, I am your friend who is Black, and not your Black friend. When I, as a Black woman, reflect on the nuances of our friendship and the keen need for me to be attentive to the dynamics of the perils of my friendship with you and countless others, I now know that "Sis" is never something you will be. I release you from the expectation to become such, and I release myself from the burden to do so under a falsely pious expectation of Christian duty in so doing. The line is clear, and that line will allow me to breathe, put my feet on the ground, and unclench my jaw. That line is a boundary worth holding on to, for the sake of my own ability to live and breathe.

I challenge myself to remember this,
to lament,
to grieve,
and to hold . . .
that "Sis" will never be it.

Perhaps, there may be a day where justice emerges more fully, allowing our cultural languages and ideologies to evolve and expand toward a more heavenly vision of the kin'dom.

But tomorrow is not yet today.
So.
We.
Wait.
How long, O Lord?

Q: Have you had any good relationships with white women?

A: But the promise . . . whose promise is it? Would I be friends with white women if I were not a Christian? Why do I pursue friendship across lines of difference anyway?

I am a reconciler. I didn't ask to be one. God shaped me into one. Can I accept the easy from God and reject the hard?

I have some relationships with white women that have truly been a balm in Gilead.

As I write this and find my system trying to regulate and soothe and heal, I just texted a friend of my heart, "I love you, Mama Faye."

Believe you me, I know Mama Faye doesn't always get it right.

But one thing she has done so far is acknowledge when she is wrong.

Mama Faye is the kind of person that if you step on her toes, she'll say, "Ouch" and thank you at the same time. "Ouch" because it hurt, but "thank you" because you just reminded her she has a bunion she needs to get checked out.

Listen, I don't know if Mama Faye has bunions or corns on her feet, but I do know that we all have healing and growing to do.

In the wake of one of the hardest sermons I've ever preached, which was effectively titled, "Dear White People," Mama Faye came to say goodbye and noted, "It wasn't easy to hear, but it needed to be said." She looked hurt, she looked pained, but somewhere within her, she took responsibility for her feelings long enough for her to hear the message and seek to be transformed; and she capped it off with the gratitude of a "thank you" that could recognize the gift of a merciful rebuke.

At that time, Mama Faye and I didn't have much of a relationship. She was just "*Ms.* Faye." The obligatory greeting for my elders.

But somewhere along the way, this white woman became Mama Faye, and I became her adopted daughter.

I love Mama Faye.

I love Sister too, and I'm still waiting for *that peril* to be turned to promise.

Q: Can anything good come out of secret meetings?

A: It wouldn't be the first time whites gathered secretly; and Black folks like me know better than to assume it's for a noble purpose.

"KIGY Brother," is America's version of "God save the King," 'cause these "American Royals" believe that their modern MAGA red caps have more jewels than white hoods, and this to them is the sound of letting freedom ring.

[Amendment by Forum Secretary: My heart grips in prayers of protection as I read these meeting minutes. I am making this amendment which has been seconded and approved following the motion to add this in, because I am pondering how these words are about to be out there in the world. I ask, do these words endanger us in any way? But I'm reminded that the prophetic mantle is her gift to steward and just like Elijah, she's not the only one. Therefore, we rebuke every Jezebel that would seek to take our lives, and the demon of white supremacy that has long wreaked havoc on our world, in the name of Jesus.]

The next time white folks decide to gather secretly in an effort to be of service to their "Black friends," maybe they'll think twice, thrice if they have to, and invite some Black folks to the table—after all, my great, great, grandfather probably built the table you've been gathering around for decades. The least we could do is invite him, his legacy, to have a seat at the table.

Q: How powerful could a seat at the table really be?

A: When I've been invited to the gathering, I've often been given the seat of honor, whether I wanted it or not.

The people who gave me this seat were seeking relationship, not another "Black friend."

It is extremely obvious when you are just someone's "Black friend," their case study, their effort to learn and meet a quota.

But real relationship has the power to heal.

Real relationship has the power to *heal.*

Q: What role does the Church play in racial reconciliation and development of real relationships?

A: I met Mama Faye at church. In the midst of her pain. In the midst of her grief. She took me in, and I received her. I received and held her, but little did she know, she took me in. We shared our lives, one to another, and from that intimate sharing and risking of vulnerability, we built a friendship that cultivated an agape love. Agape shaped a bond.

This bond was given its elements at church, but it was forged at a hearth of love, compassion, tears, and grief—the hearth that she and I had come to know as "the belly of the whale." And who knew that this whale would spit us out a little more whole than we were going in?

Q: Where has the American Church erred in manifesting God's Kingdom on earth as it is heaven?

A: Church.

The people.

The gathering place.

The work of the people.

Liturgy.

A place where Black folks have been harmed for years.

Our historical church hurt and trauma by way of exclusion is the reason the Black church exists today.

It is time for kingdom folks to do the work of repair.

Q: Are there any worthy models of racial reconciliation?

A: I needed her to talk about *it*.

I wanted her to!

She didn't.

And up until this very day, we haven't. This is not real reconciliation, rather it is sweeping the rupture under the rug.

We are living in a historical rupture.

Rupture calls for repair when possible.

Repair—root word, Old French, *reparer*.

Reparer is the foundation on which reparations stands.

The problem is most folks think reparations are a handout. *PING*. Venmo alert.

But reparation without repair defies the definition, root, and heart of the word.

The problem with the secret gathering of white women organizing DIY reparations is that they missed the mark.

This collective sin was egregious and painful.

Repentance.

Repair.

Reparations.

Reconciliation.

These R's are complicated, but I truly believe each and every one to be necessary. So often we expect reconciliation before reparation, but even Jesus's blood was offered as reparation for a breach and gave way to resurrection and reconciliation with the God of the Garden, the God who walked closely with Adam and Eve prior to the tasty delight of autumn's best Honeycrisp apple.

When I was in seminary, I felt like there were these two camps of students: those in support of reconciliation and those in support of reparations.

Vehemently at odds, one with the other, unshakeable in their conviction that one camp was more right than the other.

Reparations being for the strong and woke.

Reconciliation for they that believe in a misunderstood and popularized "kumbaya" and walking hand in hand.

This division alone defeated the essence of the shared belief that healing must come, when one without the other is cheap grace and abused mercy at best.

I will start with my Sunday School definitions and how they feed into what I know to be true for the words that don't often make it into the catechism:

Repentance: to turn away from, a 180-degree turn, to apologize sincerely to those harmed.

Repair: to fix, to return to its functioning state or better, to return to working order.

Reparations: to reimburse the cost of damages incurred. To compensate for the process of repair.

Reconciliation: to make peace and live into a unity that is worked towards after a divide that seems impossible to bring together; to bridge the gap unto the goal of repair.

Repent.

Repair.

Reparate.

Reconcile.

The task of God's people . . .

The Church.

The people.

The gathering place.

The work of the people.

Liturgy.

Somewhere amid the perils, I have had the rare opportunity to experience reconciliation. Somewhere in the midst of true and genuine relationship, things are made right, and reparations flow from a truly repentant and gracious heart.

Repair for the rupture is as beauty for ashes.

Q: Why should I stay on the battlefield? Why should I stay on the front lines of the good fight for justice?

A: For my white friends:
My sisters.
The ones who hold me down,

The ones who get under my skin,
The ones who questioned my worth,
The ones who police my Black body,
The ones who are afraid of a confident, powerful, Black woman,
Thank you.
This work is produced for us,
Because of you.
Perhaps in spite of you.
Because you've boxed us in,
Because you've been complicit,
Because you've taught me.
Some of you have loved me,
Some of you anger me,
All of you make me better.
In spite of, you.
Like sandpaper to the most beautiful, richest dark cherrywood.
You did not break me.
You made me.
Your words,
Your hate,
I overcame.

For my Black kin:
My Sistahs.
The ones who hold me down,
The ones who get under my skin,
The ones who questioned my worth,
The ones who embrace my Black body and take me in,
The ones who are completely taken by the presence and power of a confident Black woman,
Thank you.
This work is produced "for us, by us," that we might all be repairers of the breach,
Overcomers of barriers and boxes,
Repentant for the ways we've participated in one another's oppression.
That we might be committed to learning with, listening to, and loving Black women.

That our anger might be transformed righteously and crafted as more than a harmful trope,

And perhaps instead as the transformative power of *Divine* and *just* rage.

Q: Is there any hope to be found for the weary?

A: I do not know, but I pray so. I truly believe so.

May we all be better,

Like sandpaper to the most beautiful, richest, deepest, and fair tones of wood shaped into an old rugged cross, at which we may kneel and find the light.

We will not be broken,
For he was already broken for all.
Shapen in iniquity,
But molded by the Word.
May that Word,
Transform the hate that was meant for evil,
Turned for our good, that we all might surely overcome,
Someday.

Q: What are the freedom songs that will carry us through?

A: We join the cloud of witnesses in the prophetic resounding of "We Shall Overcome." We believe we shall overcome, we believe we shall be free, and we know that God will make a way.

There is room for just one final question . . .

Q: God of Salvation,
The one who reconciles us back unto thyself,
by your humbling sacrifice of putting on flesh:

Grant unto us those that would labor to be repairers of the breach and reconcilers of the heart.

For damages incurred and sacrifices made.
Give us a salve for the pain of the perilous process.
As our bodies are broken as we wait under the weight of weariness, may we trust in the promise of a world set right by you.
And may relationship be the vehicle that carries us through.

In the name of the One who lives and reigns with You, and the Holy Spirit, one God, now and forever.

Selah.

Moderator 1: The Word of God, for us the people of God.
All: Thanks be to God.
Moderator 2: All God's Children said!
All: Amen, Sis! Amen.

Notes

1. "Central Park Birdwatching Incident," Wikipedia, November 11, 2024, https://en.wikipedia.org/wiki/Central_Park_birdwatching_incident.

2. *Holy Bible, New International Version* (Biblica, Inc., 2011), Mark 7:26–28.

18

Dorena's Response

A Dance in the Morning Light

Dorena Williamson

My dear sister-friend, Kadeisha,

As I sat to write this letter, I smiled and remembered how I looked outside my patio door during our time at Collegeville. Movement by the lake had caught my eye; although our suites were next to each other, it was a private setting. So, any movement "out there" would catch my attention (not to mention, we Black girls were out in a rather remote space, and *you know* how we are!). To my surprise and delight, your dancing was the movement I saw. There is no tentative way to dance, is there? At least in the Kadeisha flow, there is only one way to dance—with your whole self. I hated to intrude on your sacred time so I only watched for a minute and, later, sheepishly admitted this, in case it was a breach of privacy. You were so gracious and pleasantly surprised (that means I was good and quiet in my observation).

I admit, not knowing you well yet, I was curious about a woman spending her downtime at a writing retreat dancing outside. The Minnesota weather was gorgeous, and the sun was beaming down on you as if the good Lord had a special spotlight on just you. That caught my eye too, as brown skin gleams so lovely in both the sunshine and the SON's shine.

Later on, you began to share, in our large group time, how dancing impacted you. I wrote down these words you shared:

Dancing felt like morning again to me.

That hit me, Sis. I didn't understand fully as dance is not my forte, but I got what you said.

Joy in the Morning

Maybe you remember this throwback worship song, "Trading My Sorrows," by Israel & New Breed. As a worship leader, I used to love ministering this song because the lyrics invite a whole-body-affirmation, a trading of sorrow for joy. As with many live-recorded worship experiences, there is a segment of proclamation between songs. Israel shared with the audience how joy comes in the morning; yet morning is not only the AM but also when you wake up. His song resonated with me and connects to the words you have spoken.

I remember being struck by how Israel invited us to reconsider the meaning of morning. And I want his proclamation to resonate with you. You are fully awake, Sis, fully alive. Your words at the retreat evoked so much meaning. And I understood that your whole body expressing herself in dance was entering into that joy in the morning.

Your essay was many things, but what I latched onto was the weeping and longing to be seen as a promise and not a project. I am thankful, Sis, oh so thankful, that God feels this pain too. His people endured so much yet He gave this promise that we get to enter into: "*Weeping may last through the night, but joy comes with the morning.*"[1]

Weeping

Oh Lord, the notifications, the words of shallow sorrow, the little somethings offered to absolve guilt. I relate so much to your frustration. To the internal weeping and anguish. I felt your words laced with love. For when we love well, we feel deeply. You have loved many white women well, and Sis, they didn't return the love. I hope with your words that perhaps a few might see themselves indicted in your forum and realize the error of their ways.

But we know, Sis, most of the white women really thought they were doing something. It made *them* feel so good to offer those words and gestures. And I am sorry that it made you feel more loss added to the trauma of our collective grief. I weep with you, for it hurts so much.

Because I also know the pain and pings of microaggressions, let me bestow some beauty for the ashes that were heaped at your feet.

Loving

You are a fountain of love. You see the best in people. That is a divine gift and enabling from above. And the beautiful thing about love is that it never fails—even if the people we love fail us. Therein is the heart of God that shines so beautifully through you.

So, keep on loving, Sis. Don't let anybody snatch the capacity to love from you. You have a wonderful husband and son who need all of you. The new adventure in the Motherland deserves all the love and embracing you have to give. The opportunity to grow new, loving friendships is within the grasp of your hands. Love is in you. It wasn't wasted on the white friends who didn't try to love you well in your pain. It is recharged within the pain, and it is bubbling up and ready to be poured out yet again!

Healing

Would you believe that I wrote down something else you said during our collective time?

We deserve to heal.

Thank you for saying those precious words. I needed that reminder of my worthiness. I also needed that permission to acknowledge the wounding that has come from my friendships with white women. Because you will not heal if you think you are unscathed by the harm of anti-Blackness from white women. Your words stirred in me the desire to reach toward that healing, just like your arms reached out in the dance I observed. Round and round, circling your arms down and then up to the sky, your posture was one of life, healing, and freedom. So, thank you for reminding me that healing is for me.

I boomerang the blessing right back to you. Not with force—for your words show the harshness of your body's response to the questioning and even taunting from white friends who demanded that you applaud their performative gestures. They really did hurt you, Sis, and I lament. I grieve. Just as your whole body moves in rhythm to the music played or felt, your whole body has suffered under the grief of these so-called friends. With the same gentleness that you soothe Kwame when he is hurting, singing over him and assuring him that he will be okay, I speak over you words of comfort.

You did not deserve the panic attacks, the demands for response, the scorning and rebuke. It is so hard when it comes from those you have loved.

And I saw in the precious time we spent together, that you are healing. You laughed loudly, spoke thoughtfully, and gestured with passion. Your body language communicated freedom and joy. The harm did not destroy you. You are still alive, and you are well.

Colorful Celebration

Because I have written about this, I must speak to the illusion of colorblindness that plagued your white friends. It is a made-up world where our delightful differences are erased. But I affirm that you—yes *you*, Kadeisha—are made in the image of God.

Every human bears the imprint of the Imago Dei. I join you in rejecting the harm of colorblindness that minimizes the glory of God that is on display in your life. I'm so glad that you are teaching your son a better way to view himself and those around him—as equally made in the very image of God and of infinite value.

Reflecting on Reconciliation

This line right here stopped me in my tracks.

> *I am a reconciler. I didn't ask to be one. God shaped me into one.*

I, too, have been shaped into a reconciler with decades of diverse ministry. And if there is one thing I know well, it's that you don't enter that kind of work lightly.

Mischaracterization is part of the lonely and difficult road of being called to reconciliation. So, I want to honor the shaping, stretching, and straining that comes with that path. I also invite you to sacred and continued rest, for ultimately, Jesus paid the price none of us could, and it is supremely His work. He will show you when to operate wisely in the ministry of reconciliation.

Along that path, it is so kind of God to graft in saints like sweet Mama Faye. I'm so proud of how you treasure that relational capital and honor her wisdom, for it says much about your integrity that you have remained under her influence while allowing her to learn from your life. How sweet it is to be able to see at least one white female friend begin to unpack and acknowledge her white fragility. Hold to the hope of Mama Faye's heart change. It is a rare treasure!

Instead of hoping to belong in places not built with you in mind, I pray you will simply create intentional spaces of safety for others who look like you. It may be dancing together, sitting on a floor with cushions, playing with dear loved ones, or enjoying robust conversation over good food and drink. You have the gift of guiding people toward freedom, hope, and healing. I know you've received a great deal of education and training, and those tools are valuable. But I also highlight your beautiful heart, moving and drawing people into safety and liberation. Here's to sitting at those created places as an elder of wisdom and strength, one whom many will look to with hearts open wide.

Repair

Your question about the church's complicity in our racial brokenness filled me with a familiar sorrow. We have, at times, been a beautiful, light-filled force of empowerment in the world and in our local context. You know the scriptures as well as I do, and within her pages are glimpses of God's people doing the good work of seeing justice roll down. But today's church, at least in the West, has lost its way. She forgot who she was and who she belonged to. And so, we see many crying peace where there is no peace. We have gaping wounds, yet many ask whatever could be wrong with us.

And yet, Sis, we cannot lose hope. From the very beginning of time, the first humans were called to cooperate with God for the flourishing of all creation. That call continues with you and me. When we get tired, let's just lift each other's hands. Let us remember that harvest comes after the patient sowing and watering. Let us embrace this call in a new way: We are repairers. We flow in the healing grace of God and look to make right what is wrong. We do so with a spirit of humility, with the foundation of wisdom, and the great cloud of witnesses who endured and who cheer us on.

We've come this far by faith. You know who we've been leaning on—the Lord! Still trusting His word. He hasn't failed us yet—and He won't.

I end by reflecting on the old spiritual,

Glory, glory hallelujah, since I laid my burdens down.
I feel better, so much better, since I laid my burdens down.[2]

I hope you felt better as you laid your burdens down by penning a part of your journey. The glory is that we do not have to bear these burdens alone. You and I both trust the God above who is the author of our story. And thanks to His immense kindness, we are now part of each other's stories.

So, dance on my sweet friend. Put on your vibrant colors and your stretchy fabrics. Lift your head to the rising sun, and feel the warmth of your God as He sings over you. Swing those arms wild and free, knowing you have all the love to give. Twist and turn, as you breathe in and out. Even your bones rejoice. Kick those legs up, Girl, proud and confident in God's good work that yet flows through your life.

Dancing in the light with you,
Dorena

Notes

1. *Holy Bible, New International Version* (Biblica, Inc., 2011), Psalm 30:5 (paraphrase)

2. "Glory, Glory Hallelujah." Hymnary.org. Accessed October 12, 2023. https://hymnary.org/text/glory_glory_hallelujah_since_i_laid_my_b.

19

When You Let Go

Reflections on Misplaced Sisterhood, Double Dutch, and Other Reasons to Drop the Rope

Velynn Brown

Slap
Slap

Hits the rope one blue, second red
Blurs of purple leaping over Afro-puffed heads

Tap
Tap

Feet moving fast—how long can our groove last?

Rock
Rock

Rapping our songs feel so good

Rock
Rock

Synched in three parts—we really getting down
Oooowweeeee Girl, did you hear that harmony sound?

Rock
Rock

~

I loved people where I first learned to love people—from my first cousin crew. We loved as big as you could blow a bazooka bubble and as long as you could keep your turn in Double Dutch.

Growing up in Oregon—one of the whitest states in the country—was like being the only chocolate chip in the cookie dough. This growing up in not just otherness but "onliness" meant my immediate family and remnant community held me close—insulating me in my very first and carefully chosen affinity circle.

I had the privilege of being, communing, and playing with my first cousins on the regular. From impromptu slumber parties at one of our aunties' or uncles' houses to dance-offs in Grand-Daddy's burnt orange and brown leather basement, I learned the bedrock of friendship: care, consistency and consideration.

You see my grandmother and her sister married brothers, making us a double set of Fraziers. Making my belonging to a family tree of over two hundred members feel proud and protected. My grandmother had five children, and her sister had five children as well. My daddy was the youngest, so when I was born, there was already a tribe of Frazier cousins making their way in our small, tight-knit community.

My cousins were everything to me. They were my first best friends—we called ourselves *sister-cousins*. Growing up was like Wakanda on the weekends and Antarctica during the week. Weekends were filled with collective care—a kind of nurturing that wrapped around me like a soft, warm blanket. My Black Utopia made my heart rise like the noonday sun—bright, bold, and glorious. But come Monday, that warmth was replaced by the sharp chill of the world outside. The safety would slip away, traded for rigid rules, frozen stares, and hearts iced over. If whiteness had a temperature, it would hover at zero degrees Celsius and falling.

Double Dutch was the most complex but favorite cousin game. We could play for hours and hours. Holding on to that rope and never letting go. We would all sing, cheering and chanting with soul conviction. If you had the ropes, you had to understand timing, tension, and keeping a steady beat. If you were the jumper, you had to know where and how long to plant your step and degree of leap.

We argued, dropped rope, competed, but never did we let go. We encouraged each other not to give up when we struggled with keeping our personal and collective rhythm. We celebrated long and hard when one of us stayed in that pocket of endless turns and no stops.

Slowly inchin' I move in close
Reigning in my fear of getting stung by those I don't know

Twack
Twack

Forward leap, I'm all in
I work so hard, I don't want my turn to end

Twack
Twack

Instead of my cousins, I play with new white friends
I try to share the Double-Dutch song I've been riding in

~

As a little Black girl growing up in the '80s, I never understood why there were so many more of them than us. And for some reason, it always seemed like they didn't like us or want us around. Even when I was within the safety and security of my cousin tribe, we had to be on alert, always looking out for each other. White folks were always staring, always glaring like we weren't supposed to be in their company. If they did smile sometimes, it looked like the Joker. Like right there on the rim of that grin was an evil brewing we would soon get a whiff of.

Our parents and elders would say things like:

"Y'all stay together, ok. Don't get separated no matter what."

"Be careful. You just can't trust them."

"It's better to stay safe than be sorry. Just keep to yourself so that way they can't mess with you."

I didn't understand why interactions with white people were deemed taboo or why my going out always seemed like this big deal or some kind of mission impossible. My elders had not participated in DEI training to have language to name and call out white supremacist culture, but they had the knowing. The knowing that could sense when to go and when not to go, when to call out injustices and when to just take one on the chin. It would be decades before my naivete caught up with the quiet ocean of calculated generational racial terror streaming right underneath me.

Yes, there really are Black people who live in Oregon. Black pioneers were among the earliest non-Native people to settle in Oregon, but it was not until World War II that thousands of African Americans migrated to the Northwest to find work in the shipyards and keep the railroads running. On faith and a flier, my grandfather Joe Frazier took his chances and left Minden, Arkansas, and did his own pioneering to the Pacific Northwest to work in the shipyard.

Today, Portland is home to more than 37,000 Black Americans,[1] most living on the east side of the Willamette River. Oregon, known for its own preference in selecting its racial makeup, didn't become a slave state or free state; it became a no-Blacks-allowed state. The 1843 Black Exclusion Law in Oregon said that Black people were not allowed to live in Oregon. Those that dared to challenge the consequence would be whipped every six months up to 39 lashes until they left the state.

This Lash Law—despite our Black community making several ignored attempts to have it removed from the state constitution—remained on the books till 2001. Today, even with the removal of a law banning the existence of Black bodies, we are splintered at the whole. We are geographically fragmented remnants of a once-thriving Black nucleus. For decades, we have not only been ignored and erased, but also predatorily displaced in the abundance of forest bathing wonder and snow-capped mountains of Portlandia. Oregon was never set up for me as a Black woman to be at home.[2]

My friendships with little white girls, and later grown white women, oftentimes started off vulnerable, genuine, loving. From sharing my favorite magenta Crayola crayon to splitting my second half of my peanut butter and jelly sandwich, I would always extend my best.

This open-hearted way of loving that understood that trust is given first rather than earned later was how I knew to move in the world. It was and, I would even offer, still is culturally, racially, and spiritually the way my people and many other Black people prefer to move in the world.

This shaping of cousin love was my blueprint for friendship. I didn't know that people let go when things got hard or difficult. I thought, like my cousins, you just admit or fix your mistakes quickly and keep it pushing.

This idea of staying connected feels both familiar and familial to me. bell hooks described friendships like this: "Loving friendships provide us with a space to experience the joy of community in a relationship where we learn to process all our issues, to cope with differences and conflict while staying connected."[3]

What I discovered in my relationships with white women that was different than my cousins was where hooks talks about the processing of all the issues. This is where there was tension, confusion, even sometimes disbelief, that what I was going through as a Black woman couldn't even be comprehended as real. Even when I had all the receipts, open wounds, undeniable evidence—that my life as a Black life did not matter—some of my closest white friends, who I thought were down, dismissed my lived experience.

~

The sequence feels off. You say it's just fine.
I tell you the rope is twisted. "Just keep going," you persisted.

Twack
Twack

My ankle gets hit; I stop to check it out.
Instead of helping, you drop the rope and pout.
I say, "Can't you see me bleeding red?
You say you can't—that I am making it all up in my head.

Throb
Throb

I ask for your help. Instead, you look me up and down.
You drop the rope and make no sound.

Throb
Throb

Like Double Dutch, I thought in my relationships with white women, we were staying in sync with our degree of vulnerability, the pacing of loyalty, one twirl after the other of memory making and promise keeping.

Looking back, I now realize that activity does not equate to authenticity. I was measuring the loyalty of these friendships on consistency rather than intimacy ("in-to-me-see"), the all and every part of me.

I had one white friend, whom I called family, ask me bluntly, "Why do you have to always bring up race? Why can't we just focus on the things we have in common—like our love for God?"

My Blackness, my lived experience of being "othered" was an inconvenience, was too much weight on our so-called "friendship." She was requiring me to disjoint, dismember, surgically remove the specific way God knit me together to be in right standing with her.

To love her and to honor our "Godly" friendship meant I had to leave all of myself and how God uniquely made me at the door.

I didn't know that sometimes people chose to walk away and not jump in because they are scared of getting hit with the rope instead of trusting that adjustments, flexibility, and trust are much more important than calling it safe and standing on the sideline.

But what I realized and learned the hard way from my closest white friendships is how you love and what you call love is different from what I offered in our relationships. I held these friendships to the sacred pedigree of sisterhood-cousinhood-family. I wasn't lacking. I wasn't begging. I was just lovingly extending myself in the centered context and values of relationship shaped by my cultural origin.[4] When you hesitated to let me sit beside you at your lunch table because I had on pro-wings and you, along with everyone at the table, were wearing penny-loafers, there was something different you were holding to measure my worth.

When you didn't believe me when I told you that our waiter came to your side first and refused to look my way, I learned very quickly that when I share what I'm experiencing and you can't see it, not only is it not real, my words are also invisible.

When I could barely afford the gas to your big party and even bigger house and brought an affordable bottle of Trader Joe's wine, the way you looked into my hands before you looked in my eyes, I realized that my presence wasn't the present, and nothing I could ever give you would be enough.

Throb
Throb

When you disagreed with me that you got the agent and book contract because you are white, and I didn't get a book contract because the same agent told me, "My experience was too Black and that there was not a market for my words," you said I just needed to put in my work, and that maybe, it wasn't God's timing. I realized then that maybe we were serving two different Gods.

My heart is on the ground.

It takes years to pick it up.
It takes years to pick it up.
It takes years to pick it up.

It became too hard to find a common rhythm, a steady cadence, a balanced flow in my relationships with white women because we were literally dancing to the beat of different drums.

And even then, I would extend myself one more time again and do these "maybe I'll try," "turn the other cheek," "just one more time" dives . . . Not because I was desperate or needy, but simply because I was willing to lay aside my way so you could fully be you. Yea, even at the expense of me. In Christian circles in particular, I too often checked my Black card at the door so that we could meet in the middle of our shared identity in Christ. I'm embarrassed to say that this is what I thought racial reconciliation looked like. This skinning off who God fully made me to be for your comfort and for my need, at the time, to be accepted is another form of emotional slavery and internalized racial oppression. I no longer subscribe to this white-centric-God Christian-empire identity. It became too much to shrink for you to shine—too much work to minimize my own worth for you to take full stage of every conversation, every decision, every detail of our relationship.

I needed a money-back guarantee to the wear and tear and warranty of my heart. It became dysfunctional—unhealthy, harmful and traumatic—to try. Do I still have friendships with white women? Christian white women? I'm sad to say I only have a few: the real-really-not-going-to-let-go-of-the-rope white folks. I call them "the ones" that remained. And, yes, they are less than what I can count on one hand. But that's ok.

What I'm realizing in what makes these relationships work or why they are different is that there has not yet been any conflict. My experience is that white women don't do well with being called into accountability. They don't do well with holding Black women's truth and experience of them.

These few that remain do not center our friendship from a white-centered view. They do not require me to whiten up my lived experience to ease their discomfort or normalize their privilege. And as I write these words I have to say, these days, I even keep those who

I consider close at a distance—because even on their best days, there has also been harm.

I would offer to Black women trying to restore friendships with white women again to go slow and be selective. It's always going to be a risk. It's worth keeping your heart open and free to love as big and as wide as it can within margins and boundaries you set. I don't want bitterness and fear to keep me—to keep us—from our big, beautiful hearts. At the same time, there must be balance. Our bodies and hearts grow weary in our extended generosity. We are exhausted from holding up white woman. We must listen to our hearts, listen to the whispers, the knowings, the gut checks.

We must guard and protect our hearts *first*.

There are terms such as *white fragility*, *cognitive dissonance*, *white shame* and *guilt*, *gaslighting*, *defensiveness*, *blame*. The list is long and wide. If you are white and reading these pages, this is your work, not mine, to unpack. But let me tell you something: These words became my Marie Kondo order and understanding of overstuffed trauma and the boxed-up horrors of racial offenses.

I needed both the definitions and Jesus. I needed the words to locate the trauma and unpack the severity and depth of the racially motivated injuries I had endured. I needed to lean into a brown Jesus. One who, as Howard Thurman would describe, stood side by side with those who "had their backs against the wall."[5] I needed God's presence and power to heal my kumbaya-conditioned heart and give me permission to speak the truth about white-supremacist culture destroying my heart and contaminating the church.

To clarify, there is nothing wrong with striving for unity and racial reconciliation. To know me is to know how hard and long I strived for a shared oneness in our humanity. I am a daughter of a Promise Keeper.[6] My father was one of the founding national leaders of the movement. I had the privilege of praying under stadiums and leading worship in pulpits, witnessing the beauty and wholeness of God embodied in centering all races representing the Imago Dei. Many decades after serving in the movement, my father told me he wished the focus would have been reparations not just reconciliation.

Faith and Equity[7] have become the grounding forces in my journey to bring together the fullness of my Black woman self and my Christ-following self—two intertwined ropes of my truest identity, now moving in a steady rhythm and deep sync. In choosing to boldly embrace both, I stepped into the complex tension of unraveling the threads of whiteness wound into Christianity, centering justice and liberation as my God-given birthright. In this space, I found the healing I had long sought, where the Gospel's true essence of freedom and equality resonated with my spirit. Through this lens, I could reclaim my identity fully, liberated and whole in faith that values Black dignity and divinely bestowed worth.

Yet, as I pursue alignment with a life of ease, belonging, and safety, I am drawn ever more to Black-centered spaces, where my identity feels affirmed and uplifted. My work at the Black Parent Initiative[8] and in launching Roots and Remnant,[9] my racial affinity consulting firm, has deepened my dedication to creating and protecting spaces where Black healing and affirmation are at the core. These spaces are both a form of spatial justice and public safety—especially in a state where Black existence is so often confined to the margins. To be seen, heard, and valued within Black spaces is, in itself, a restorative act, offering an oasis of belonging that stands against the backdrop of systemic exclusion.

In this calling, centering Black community is more than a career choice; it's a practice of resistance and reclamation. By normalizing Black space and amplifying Black voices, I work to cultivate environments that protect, nurture, and celebrate Black lives. It's a sacred undertaking to build spaces where others can find belonging and wholeness, spaces that echo the liberation God intends for us all. Spaces to be counted in, held, and celebrated—not just parts but the whole of us—which began in me first becoming whole to me.

What I'm realizing is that most white people are not coming to make things right. I've decided to stop waiting for them to step back in because the waiting drains my precious energy, health, and time. Many are not prepared for the heavy, messy work of true restorative justice; more often than not, they seek relief from shame, guilt, or frustration. When I no longer lift their emotional weight, I find they have no use for my friendship. I can't do this anymore—my time and heart are too valuable to keep investing in friendships that leave me unmatched and unfulfilled.

I'm also no longer seeking acceptance from white people—that's too much power to give anybody. I no longer need their apologies, their permission, or any validation of my worth. I'm striving to belong wholly to God and myself now. I no longer need anyone else to hold my rope.

This time no longer two ropes, it's just one and no friends
I'd rather play alone and celebrate myself
Then get dissed by white folk when I ask for their help
I'm not waiting on the corner for them to come back to me . . .

I've learned to sing my own song while jumping through a single rope. It gets a little lonely sometimes, but the solitude is much healthier and easier to manage than the danger of being sliced away alive with the daily dose of hundreds of paper-thin micro and macro cuts.

In fact, I'm building a new bus with those who remain faithful and stay
Who believed me when I say what I say
I've even reached back to those old Cousin days.

As I write this essay, I am on Southwest Airlines headed to Houston, Texas with my now-adulting cousin circle. We are celebrating my first cousin's "It's giving 50th" birthday. Twelve deep in all, the Black Girls. We are dressed in red and denim. We have laughed so hard we have shaken the plane. Instead of Double Dutch, there will be wobbling, electric sliding, and cha-chas. And even after all this time, I'm in awe and so relieved that they never once let go.

I've picked up the rope again
I've picked back up my rope again
I've picked back up our rope again

These spaces are my home again, my oxygen.
Here is where I learned to let go—so I could grab and finally hold all of me.

Notes

1. "U.S. Census Bureau Quickfacts: Portland City, Oregon," QuickFacts Portland city, Oregon, accessed October 28, 2024, https://www.census.gov/quickfacts/portlandcityoregon.

2. To learn more, please visit the Vanport Mosaic Project (https://www.vanportmosaic.org/community-gatherings) and The Oregon Black Pioneers (https://oregonblackpioneers.org/). Please also read *Vanport (Images of America)* by Zita Podany (Arcadia Publishing, 2016).

3. bell hooks, *All About Love* (New York: William Morrow, an imprint of HarperCollins Publishers, 2018), 133–134.

4. Dr. Edwin Nichols's framework of axiology (study of values) and epistemology (study of knowing) would normalize my African diasporic view of friendship: A world where the highest value lies in the relationships between persons. This research would also help me put into context why persons of European descent's highest values are centered around objects or the acquisition of objects. Edwin Nichols, "The Philosophical Aspects of Cultural Difference," Academia.edu, July 30, 2017, https://www.academia.edu/34081061/The_Philosophical_Aspects_of_Cultural_Difference.

5. Howard Thurman, *Jesus and the Disinherited* (Boston: Beacon Press, 1996), 11.

6. Promise Keepers is an Evangelical Christian parachurch organization for men, founded in 1990 by Bill McCartney. "Promise Keepers vision is that every man—regardless of denomination, generation, race, or culture—has the opportunity to receive new life, know God's Word, and follow Christ in Kingdom changemaking." "About Us—Promise Keepers," Promise Keepers, September 24, 2023, https://promisekeepers.org/about-us/.

7. Faith and Equity Collective was sponsored and supported by cofounder Hanif Fazal and the Center For Equity and Inclusion.

8. Black Parent Initiative (BPI) is a culturally-specific, community-rooted organization that co-designs innovative, sustainable supports with Black families, guided by Dr. Joy DeGruy's 3M Relationship Approach, community-centered design, and continuous improvement strategies.

9. To learn more about Roots and Remnant, please visit velynnmbrown.com.

20
Deidra's Response

Rope Burns

Deidra Riggs

Games

When I am five years old, I lay prone in the middle of the street in front of our little yellow house and press the left side of my face into the sun-soaked asphalt—a chunk of sheetrock chalk in my hand. At the end of our road, a construction crew has left behind a gigantic pile of sheet rock and electrical wire, and we neighborhood kids believe we've discovered a treasure chest of toys instead of a heap of debris discarded and forgotten. We are the redeemers. We've harvested the sheet rock, and we've used our mothers' kitchen shears to snip long cords of electrical wire to repurpose for our own important projects.

If you take a chunk of sheet rock and peel off the paper casing, you're left with a chunk of chalk, and we use that to draw roadways for our Matchbox cars. We draw hopscotch boxes and sprawl our bodies on the ground while a playmate from the neighborhood traces our likeness on the street. I lay prone on the asphalt, the warmth from the road anointing the left side of my face. We liberate the electrical wires from their plastic sheath and separate the individual pieces ("What color do you want?" "I want red!" "Purple! Can I have purple?" "Is this blue?" "No, I think it's called turquoise." "Turquoise. Yeah. That. I want turquoise."), and we braid it to make rings and bracelets and earrings for our Barbie dolls.

When I am nine, I learn to jump Double Dutch. We jump in the middle of that same asphalt road from sunup to sundown. "Down, down baby, down by the roller coaster . . ." We high step, and we turn around, and we touch the ground, and we count how many times we can jump without missing while the ropes turn faster and faster like a hand mixer on high speed. Turning the ropes is as important as jumping. No one has to tell us just how much we need each other if it's going to work. We cheer each other on and high-five each other for finally getting it or jumping the fastest or the lowest or the longest or just jumping at all. We know we are fire. We feel it. In our bones.

When I am thirteen, we ride our bicycles in the streets with no hands—arms stretched out until our fingers touch and we are a single, unbroken wave of absolute glory, spanning the entire width of the road. Our cornrows and afros and hot combed hairdos bob and weave like halos of butterflies against bluebird skies. We sing Sister Sledge and Evelyn "Champagne" King and Gladys Knight and *always always always* Aretha (surely you don't need me to say her last name, do you?). *Slay, Queens, slay!*

When I am eighteen, I go to college, and every night, we play Spades until three o'clock in the morning. We are raucous and hilarious, and we do. not. play. We look at our partner across the table, we dip our chin, and we raise an eyebrow and say we have six and a possible seven, and we absolutely mean what we say. We may be bluffing, or hoping against hope, but we are not lying. We are straight up sending telepathic messages to our partner through our foreheads and our eyeballs, and they know we know that we know, and we know they know, too. We collect our books with a lean, and we trash talk, and we slam our cards on the table, and we might even fall out of our chairs, and it's always best when the RA is Black and joins our games, so no one has to listen to complaints about the noise on this particular floor of any particular dormitory at this specific PWI.

When I am grown, I kick off my shoes at the family reunion and the bridal reception and the baby shower and the church barbecue, and I do the Electric Slide and the Cupid Shuffle and the Wobble with my sisters and my Aunties and my Uncles and my cousins who I just met and aren't actually related but now we are inseparable, and we are fire, and we were born with the groove in our hearts, and so we *walk it by yourself* exactly on the beat and with flair, together on the parquet floor.

Yesterday, when I cross the street after eating chicken and waffles in the restaurant with my mom, I spy a Sister crossing the other way and

I shout out, "Okay, hair! I see you!" She smiles and waves and points at me, and she does a little spin right then and there, and I wink back, and the universe smiles at us forever.

Double Dutch

Double Dutch is Black girls' jazz. And that's the root of our Black Girl Magic.[1]

Legend has it that Double Dutch came to America by way of Dutch colonists. It's hard to say where the game originated. But what we do know is when Black girls in urban areas like Harlem and Bed-Stuy took up the ropes, Double Dutch became a whole vibe.

I learned Double Dutch from the older girls on my cul-de-sac. They patiently cheered me on and gave me pointers on how to judge correctly the right moment to jump into the space created between those two churning ropes, just missing each other, like the beaters on my mother's blender when she mixed pound cake batter in the bowl in the kitchen. Just like those beaters, I did not want to get caught in the mix of the ropes at the wrong moment.

Anyone who's jumped Double Dutch on a sidewalk in the summertime knows the slap-slap sound of those two ropes hitting the concrete as they finish their downward arc and start toward the skies on their way back around. Jumping with one rope was a skill, but Double Dutch? Jumping Double Dutch is an art.

Double Dutch is a dance performed by three or more people, with two ropes. Turning the rope is just as critical as the actual act of jumping over those two ropes, crisscrossing each other right beneath your feet (if, hopefully, you timed it right). The two people turning the rope have got to be in sync with each other. Think what you want, but when the jumper is in the midst of the vortex of those two ropes, so much of her success depends on just how much those rope turners know what they're doing, and just how much those rope turners truly want her to succeed.

You wouldn't know it just to look at it, but the rope turning matters more than you know.

I never had anyone drop the rope on me when I jumped Double Dutch. Dropping the rope as a rope turner, especially if someone was in the ropes jumping? Absolutely unheard of. Unacceptable. A betrayal on so many levels. You cannot drop the rope without somebody suffering the consequences.

As a rope turner, you never pull that rope up short, either. You don't scratch your nose. You don't swat at a fly. You don't wave hi to that cute one over there. You turn the rope. Because you're invested. It's a game. But also? We do not play.

When it was my chance to be the rope turner, I always loved it if we were using one of those super long sections of clothesline that somebody's mama had picked up at the five and dime. I mean, even back then, something about having one long piece of rope instead of two shorter ones intrigued me. And my favorite thing of all was when we took that long piece of rope and tied a knot in it so that it was one gigantic circle of rope.

When that happened . . . ? When *that* happened, the rope turners stepped inside that circle of rope. We hitched the rope up over our hips and held it right at our waists. Then, we stepped back so there was just the right amount of slack in the rope. We locked eyes, we glued our feet to the ground, we took a piece of rope in each hand, and then, slowly at first—one hand and then the other—we started turning those two ropes until the slap slap sound on the concrete blended with the whir of the ropes as they cut through the air. Once the stage was set, all eyes were on the jumper.

The jumper stood just outside the ropes. She usually had one foot in front of the other, her hands up in front of her, swaying forward and back with her eyes on those ropes, waiting for just the right moment to make . . . her . . . move, and then—well, if you know, you know.

It was magic.

Solitaire

You know the game of solitaire, don't you? It's just you and a deck of cards. The name of the game says it all. It's meant to be played alone. Velynn's essay is a journey from learning to trust through the pain of learning not everyone can be trusted, to deciding to count on herself. I think so many of us have been there. For Black women, a lot of the lessons about who not to trust have, unfortunately, come through our interactions, relationships, friendships, and acquaintances with white women.

I don't think anyone reading this essay would deny they've been hurt by all kinds of women, but the scenarios Velynn offers highlight the uniquenesses of the betrayals of Black women's white counterparts. Whether gaslighting us, minimizing who we are, or invalidating and nullifying our lived experiences outright, white women clearly don't know the gravity of dropping the rope or pulling up short. They don't understand how their unwillingness to lock in to the moment, turn the rope, and commit to one another leaves rope burns on all of us.

Historically, those rope burns have been seared into the necks of the strange fruit Billie Holiday sang about. The rope burns have looked like Jim Crow and redlining and signs that say, "For Whites Only." The rope burns have been chiseled into the headstones of Sandra Bland and Breonna Taylor—and do you really need me to name the rest and all of those who loved them? Love them.

White women, you are playing strange games with yourselves. Your rules are nebulous. Your acting at fair play is unconvincing. Your unwillingness to commit, to lock eyes, to dig in your heels, and to turn the damn rope is all we really need to see to know for sure. And so, at the end of her essay, Velynn chooses a solitary rope; a solitary game. I can feel the ache in her soul as I read her beautiful words. I can feel the bewilderment in the questions she asks. *Did that just happen? Is that what I think it is? Is it me?* Her *set-apart-ness*, is palpable. At first, it might look like loneliness, but it's not that. Not at all, because we know we are not ever alone in this world. Black women are descendants of kings and queens. We are beloved. We are chosen and we are magic. And in biblical terms, set-apart-ness is the very same thing as sanctified.

I looked up the word solitaire, just to be sure I wasn't missing anything, because I do know the rest of the story, but I know I need to be sure for something like this that will go in a book. And so, let me leave it here, in black in white:

> *solitaire*
> noun
> sol·i·taire ˈsä-lə-ˌter
> 1: a single gem (such as a diamond) set alone[2]

A single gem. This is the magic of Black women. We are jewels. Whether alone, or set in gold or platinum alongside so many more Black gems, we know our value; we know what we are worth. It is not on us if white women can't see it; can't celebrate it. What is that to us? Whose loss is that? Not ours, to be sure.

Come on, my beautiful Black Sister. We are here to turn the rope for you. We are committed. We are locked in. We are in sync. We are for you. We are with you. You will not get burned here. Jump in.

Notes

1. "Double Dutch: Jump In!," The Kennedy Center, accessed September 18, 2023, https://www.kennedy-center.org/education/resources-for-educators/classroom-resources/media-and-interactives/media/hip-hop/double-dutch-jump-in/.

2. "Solitaire Definition & Meaning," *Merriam-Webster*, accessed September 18, 2023, https://www.merriam-webster.com/dictionary/solitaire.

Wonder Beyond Wounds

A Collective Poem

For Every Black Woman and Girl Journeying Toward Healing and Home

WORDS WRITTEN BY THE *WE DESERVE TO HEAL* CONTRIBUTORS
ARRANGED AND SHAPED BY VELYNN BROWN

May you hold close the courage of those who dreamed you'd exist,
Africa's daughters beautifully sun-kissed.
Each time you inhale joy and exhale peace,
Fill yourself full with love, let your soul release.

In silence, find whispers, in stillness, find grace,
A sacred foundation, no one can replace.
Let instinct be armor, a gift and a guide,
Feel the strength of your knowing, no need to compromise.

Marvel at your own magic; shine bright, let them see,
That you're woven in wonder, whole and free.
You are a stardust blessing that never grows old.
Galaxy of possibility, the brightest diamond without a mold.

Find sacred places where your soul can fly high,
Where beauty, dancing, and dreams are alive.
Trust the quiet voice that rises from within—
Never be ashamed of who you are or where you've been.

Wounds meant to destroy; with time give confidence,
To know whom to choose and whom to leave on the fence.
Feel the pulse of your ancestors in each beat of your heart,

A tapestry woven, each thread tells a story
Of how you'll get over and shine your own glory.

Dream with a heart unweighted by approval and greed.
Do what makes you come alive—let that become seed.
To harvest and gather till your heart is made full,
Share with others abundance from your own plate
That no one can steal, that no one can take.

May play scatter freely, like sun on your skin,
May love find you wholly, deeply within.
Let ease bring treasures, hidden and true,
For rest is a birthright, a gift to renew.

Your body is perfect, your spirit divine—
When God made you, God took abundant time.
Move in the truth that only you know,
For in your own light, true beauty does show.
Just as you are, a wonder, a grace,
A blessing unmeasured, no one can erase.

May laughter find you, may warmth abound,
With friends who lift you, your tribe will be found,
A bond of sisterhood both tried and true.
Stretching and growing the best inside of you.
This way of friendship is steady and wide,
A place where safety, blessing, and reverence abide.

Worthy are you of all that is good,
Of bliss and joy, of love understood.
No tear will be wasted, every dream will be grown,
The life you imagined—the place you'll call home.

You owe no answers, no reasons to give,
Your truth is your truth, and yours to live.
Walk tall and proud, let your smile beam,
Be free to rest, to weep, to stand,
To hold or release with an open hand.

Shoulders unburdened, no weight to bear,
For you need not be a bridge everywhere.

Find solace in stepping back when you choose,
In trusting the strength that comes from you.
For wisdom is yours first to carry within,
Don't ignore what it tells you the first time—lean in.

Shine without shrinking, fierce in your joy,
Honored and cherished, without any ploy.
Each laugh, each smile, a blessing so clear,
A testament to all who brought you here.

Bask in your radiance, powerful, true,
A light that is sacred, crafted anew.
Fearfully made, as you boldly show—
A wonder, a beauty, a radiant glow.

A Note from Velynn Brown about the making of "Wonder Beyond Wounds"

This collective verse exercise invited each essayist in this anthology to give voice to their personal needs, hopes, and dreams while also sharing wishes, cautions, and blessings for Black women and young Black girls—past, present, and future—as they navigate the deep challenges of white supremacy and the complexities of relationships with white women. In this sacred time together, I sought to capture the spirit, the voices, and the witnessing that unfolded as we reflected on our journeys and experiences. This poem is a love letter—first to ourselves, then to all Black women who will read our words and find resonance within them.

Acknowledgments

Gratitude from the Editor

Before I begin, let me thank you, dear reader, for taking time to read these words and feel the emotions that may arise from engaging with this book. If you believe it matters that more people know about this book, you are welcome to leave a review in all the places AND to tell someone else about *We Deserve to Heal*. Thank you!

First and foremost, I am filled with such love, joy, and deep wells of gratitude when I think of each of the contributors to this project: Dorena Williamson, Chichi Agorom, Deidra Riggs, Kathryn V. Stanley, Oluwatomisin Olayinka Oredein, Paula Owens Parker, Quantrilla Ard, Kadeisha M. Bonsu, and Velynn Brown. This work would not have been possible without each of you. I know that crafting these essays was a tremendous emotional undertaking. I cannot thank each of you enough for your willingness to take your questions and curiosity to the page—despite the struggles you encountered. And thank you, as well, for all the support you have each offered me along the way. Yes, I may have been the editor of this project, but we created something remarkable together.

Immense gratitude to my agent Keely Boeving. Writers need people in their lives who believe in the importance and value of their work. Thank you for being such a person for me. Thank you also to editor extraordinaire Abby Freeland. Our first call spilled over with such excitement, and I knew this book would have a good home with University Press of Kentucky. Thank you also to Abby's UPK colleagues, including Gale Greenlee, Katie Gibson Cross, Ila McEntire, Leanna Dean, and Jackie Wilson. Thank you for the care and attention UPK has given this book. It's been wonderful working with each of you.

Thank you to the Louisville Institute for offering me and so many others the resources to explore ideas that have the power to change our world for good. Receiving a grant from you launched this work and empowered me to take another step and another step and another step. Thank you to the Collegeville Institute. You have long been a meaningful part of my writing journey. Your interest in hosting all the contributors for an in-person gathering transformed the nature of this project in the best way possible. Thank you for such a beautiful invitation beyond anything I could have asked or imagined. Thank you to the Arts and Science Council of Charlotte Mecklenburg County. An Artist Support Grant enabled me to attend AWP 2024, where I first connected with the University Press of Kentucky! The ways you support artists in our community is awe-inspiring. Thank you for your work.

Thank you so much to anyone who heard me speak about this project and said some version of "I want to read that book" or "I need that book." Such responses reminded me that this project carried with it the potential to change lives. Much gratitude to Stina Kielsmeier-Cook who helped me think through applying for a Louisville Institute Pastoral Study Project grant *and* took time to read my application. Thanks for that initial enthusiasm that served as a place to start. Thank you to Kadeisha, Tomi, Tamara Burdon, Roohi Choudhry, Addie K. Sanders, and Denise Flanders. Your reminders of the importance of this work, your willingness to think through ideas with me, and your pointed encouragement to care for myself in this process have been generous, life-giving acts that have helped sustain me.

A special word of gratitude to my daughters. Motherhood has shaped my writing journey and my life in countless ways steeped in joy, beauty, and goodness. Surely, life is not easy, but to look at you is to embrace possibility. Your mama loves you with her whole heart. And Nyasha, words of thanks can't convey all that you've added to these past years. You know more than anyone that this journey from initial idea to published book has been a long, tangled one. My Love, you have encouraged me and held me and listened to me and believed for me—with this book and across this life. All my gratitude. I love you with my whole heart.

Finally, to the One who planted this idea, watered it, and created the space for it to grow. Thank you for this invitation to participate in the making of what might offer healing. Stewarding this work has been an honor.

Contributors

Chichi Agorom is a writer, educator, and facilitator. She is the author of *The Enneagram for Black Liberation*, host of the podcast *From Armor to Ease*, a certified Enneagram teacher and core faculty at the Narrative Enneagram, and a former psychotherapist whose life's work is to support people on their journeys toward wholeness and healing. Her greatest joy is learning how to belong to herself, and creating spaces—physically and with her words—that help others feel less alone and more known. Visit her website at chichiagorom.com.

Quantrilla Ard resides with her family in the Atlanta area. Her goal is to encourage women in all stages of life through empathy, transparency, and love. She is a faith-based personal and spiritual development author, dynamic speaker, people-connector, and grief coach who believes in the power of collective strength, community, and fellowship. She holds a doctoral degree in health psychology and is a champion for social and reproductive justice with a focus on Black maternal/infant health and mortality. You can follow her work and journey at thephdmamma.com.

Kadeisha M. Bonsu is a God-chaser, wife, and mother. By vocation she is a psychotherapist and ordained minister, but by design she is a spiritual midwife, racial reconciler, cultural translator, and wounded healer. Kadeisha is a lover of words, written and embodied, and through those creative gifts, she communicates healing. She is currently working on her first book, a memoir about the intersections of motherhood, faith, and mental health. You can learn more about her at kadeishabonsu.com.

Velynn Brown is founder of Roots and Remnant, a consulting firm focused on Black liberation and racial healing. She serves as the chief director of programs and operations at the Black Parent Initiative, where she advocates for social justice by providing innovative strategies to address systemic inequalities, with an emphasis on holistic healing and sustainable transformation. Velynn, also a spoken-word poet, is currently working on her first published collection. She enjoys gospel music, deep conversations, traveling the world, and cherishing time with her husband, children, grandchildren, and close friends. Learn more at velynnmbrown.com.

Oluwatomisin Olayinka Oredein is Assistant Dean for Strategic Initiatives and Theological Imagination and associate professor in Black religious traditions and constructive theology and ethics at Brite Divinity School in Fort Worth, Texas. Her creative and scholastic work engages liminal identity and faith, American African explorations in womanism, theopoetics, constructive theology, and social ethics. She is the author of *The Theology of Mercy Amba Oduyoye: Ecumenism, Feminism, and Communal Practice*, coeditor of *Theopoetics in Color: Embodied Approaches in Theological Discourse*, and the author of a forthcoming work on the theological ethics of care. Visit her website tomioredein.com for more!

Paula Owens Parker is passionate about healing generational trauma in the African American community, spirituality, and womanist mysticism, and she has spoken in conferences, retreat centers, churches, and seminary classrooms nationally and internationally. She is a Presbyterian clergywoman and author of *Roots Matter: Healing History, Honoring Heritage, Renewing Hope* and chapters in *Kaleidoscope: Broadening the Palette in the Art of Spiritual Direction* and *Walking through the Valley: Womanist Explorations in the Spirit of Katie Geneva Cannon.* She lives in Virginia. Visit her website: PaulaOwensParker.com.

Deidra Riggs is a writer, speaker, and spiritual strategist who tells the truth with tenderness. Her work invites readers to come home to themselves and to the sacred beauty of everyday life. She is the author of several books, including *Every Little Thing* and *One: Unity in a Divided World*, and her essays often explore the intersections of faith, family, memory, and personal freedom. Deidra lives in Connecticut, where she honors the small things that shape a life—and chooses with care what to carry forward, and what to let go. Follow her on Instagram @ deidrariggs or visit her website, DeidraRiggs.com.

Kathryn V. Stanley is an Atlanta-based fifth-generation educator, public theologian, writer, and editor who uses her gifts to support others in finding their voices. Her own writing has appeared in both scholarly and creative spaces and reflects stories from her ancestors. Kathryn is a graduate of Spelman College and Candler School of Theology, and has been a Black Theology and Leadership Institute fellow at Princeton Seminary. She is a part of the Christian education leadership team at Ebenezer Baptist Church and has also served as a writing coach and fellow at the Collegeville Institute. Her forthcoming book, *Raising Faithful Advocates*, explores spiritual formation among African American youth. Find her at raisingfaithfuladvocates.wordpress.com.

Dorena Williamson is a longtime bridge-builder, church planter, pastor, and best-selling author of multiple children's books, including *ColorFull*, *Crowned with Glory*, *The Story of Juneteenth*, and *Brown Baby Jesus*. Her writing has been featured in *Christianity Today* and Barna, and she has spoken in conferences and classrooms nationwide. She is passionate about using the power of story to help children honor and celebrate their fellow image-bearers. She and her family make their home near Nashville, Tennessee. Visit her at dorenawilliamson.com.

About the Editor

Patrice Gopo is an award-winning essayist who writes words that touch wounds and speak to the hope of healing. Her essay collections include *Autumn Song*, recipient of the inaugural Pattis Family Foundation Creative Arts Book Award, and *All the Colors We Will See*, a Barnes & Noble Discover Great New Writers selection. Patrice lives with her family in North Carolina, where she enjoys walks just after dawn and thinks a perfect day ends with ice cream. Please visit patricegopo.com to learn more.